THE BEST FRIENDS' GUIDE TO

PREGNANCY AND MOTHERHOOD

Daily Diary

VICKI IOVINE

BLOOMSBURY

The author of this book is not a physician and the ideas, procedures, and suggestions in this book are not intended as a substitute for the medical advice of a trained health professional. All matters regarding your health require medical supervision. Consult your physician before adopting the suggestions in this book, as well as about any condition that may require diagnosis or medical attention. The author and publisher disclaim any liability arising directly or indirectly from the use of this book.

First published in Great Britain 1997
This edition published 2005
Bloomsbury Publishing Plc, 38 Soho Square, London W1D 3HB

First published in the USA 1997
Pocket Books, a division of Simon & Schuster Inc.
1230 Avenue of the Americas, New York, NY 10020

ISBN 0 7475 8062 6

10 9 8 7 6 5 4 3 2 1

Interior illustrations by Lesley Ehlers

All papers used by Bloomsbury Publishing are natural, recyclable products made from wood grown in well-managed forests. The manufacturing processes conform to the environmental regulations of the country of origin.

Typeset by Hewer Text Composition Services, Edinburgh
Printed in China by Tims Printing

www.bloomsbury.com/vickiiovine

DEDICATED WITH LOVE

To GramAndrea, who forced me to take typing in high school, but who still types faster than I do. Thanks for overlooking some of my exaggerations, for loving our kids, and for working as hard as I did to meet my deadline.

– AND –

To Jody, who became every aspect of me except author so that I could work without being noticeably absent, and who has such a powerful smile you can feel it as well as see it.

INTRODUCTION

Never has a day been more anxiously anticipated than the birth of your baby. As a kid, you probably thought there were several light-years between holidays. Getting your driving licence felt like it took forever to finally happen, as did your graduation, your twenty-first birthday and maybe even your engagement. Small potatoes next to the journey of a woman who has gone from missing her period to becoming the mother of a child.

Every day for the next year will be surprising, confusing, thrilling, tedious, nerve-racking and hopefully not too nauseating, but you are not alone because *The Best Friends' Guide to Pregnancy Daily Diary* is here for you all the way, and we won't desert you after the birth.

You'll learn quickly that the greatest myth of pregnancy is that it lasts nine months. Average gestation is forty weeks, which even with this new maths stuff sounds like ten months to us.

The Diary is organized to be appropriate to your transformation through all four trimesters of pregnancy: the three when the baby is inside you, and the fourth, when you're still in a pregnant state but the baby is outside you. Snippets of information, suggestions for coping, top ten lists and some good belly laughs are given in daily doses, keeping in mind the pregnancy rules of thumb regarding information: 'Don't give us more than we can handle at any given time,' or 'If you tell us too much, we'll just forget it anyway.'

Keep some notes, mark some milestones, record information from visits to the clinic, but most of all, truly enjoy this time because, in the end, it's over before you know it.

TOP 10 GREATEST LIES ABOUT PREGNANCY

10. LAMAZE WORKS.
9. MORNING SICKNESS IS GONE BY LUNCHTIME.
8. MATERNITY CLOTHES ARE SO MUCH CUTER NOW.
7. YOU WILL HAVE YOUR PREPREGNANCY FIGURE BACK IN THREE MONTHS, ESPECIALLY IF YOU BREASTFEED.
6. OIL MASSAGES PREVENT STRETCH MARKS.
5. PREGNANT WOMEN HAVE THE MOST BEAUTIFUL SKIN AND HAIR.
4. 'I SWEAR, YOUR FACE HASN'T CHANGED AT ALL!'
3. PREGNANCY BRINGS A MAN AND WOMAN CLOSER TOGETHER (YEAH, YOU AND YOUR DOCTOR!).
2. 'YOU HAVEN'T PUT ON WEIGHT ANYWHERE BUT YOUR BELLY!'
1. PREGNANCY ONLY LASTS NINE MONTHS.

DATE _____

Yippee! You are going to have a baby! Welcome to the club of mothers.
There is nothing the world loves more than a pregnant woman. The
countdown begins as you embark on what remains of the approximately
280 days it takes to cook a baby.

Now, mark the date of your last period on this page, since that's how
medical people measure how pregnant you are. In other words, you may
already be four or even six weeks pregnant. Think about it, you already
have at least a month under your belt, so to speak, and it was a piece of
cake . . . only nine more to go.

Notes:

_____

_____

_____

_____

_____

_____

DATE _____

Mark here the date of conception.

You may know when 'it' happened through good old-fashioned intuition, or you can count 14 days after your last period and mark that as the Big Event.

A few juicy details wouldn't hurt . . . you know how nosy we Best Friends can be.

NOTES

_____
_____
_____
_____
_____
_____

FIRST TRIMESTER 252 DAYS TO GO

DATE _ _ _ _ _ _ _ _ _ _ _ _ _

Congratulations . . . again!!! Now that we know you're pregnant, let's begin the countdown. For consistency's sake, let's assume you took the pregnancy test on the day your always-dependable-28-day-cycle period was supposed to start. And, to complete the fantasy, let's pretend that day was *today*.

Mark this page with today's date.

Notes

_____

_____

_____

_____

_____

_____

DATE _____

Are you still comatose, or have you leapt into that hyperactive glee of someone with a huge secret to share? Normal reactions to positive pregnancy test results span a spectrum of emotions from absolute terror, through dazed ambivalence, to euphoria, so don't second-guess your feelings. In fact, do yourself a favour and try out all the possible emotions just to get the full pregnancy experience.

Mark today's date on this page, and tomorrow's date on the next page, and so on. There, now we've got the rhythm.

NOTES

_____

_____

_____

_____

_____

_____

TOP 10 REASONS TO SUSPECT YOU'RE PREGNANT

10. YOUR BREASTS ARE BIGGER, PUFFIER AND A LOT MORE SENSITIVE.

9. YOU NEED TO URINATE FREQUENTLY, ESPECIALLY IN THE MIDDLE OF THE NIGHT.

8. YOU'RE EVEN MORE EXHAUSTED THAN USUAL.

7. PHANTOM PERIOD PAINS – YOU SWEAR YOUR PERIOD IS ABOUT TO START.

6. YOU'RE DIZZY AND LIGHT-HEADED, AND YOU MAY EVEN FAINT.

5. NAUSEOUS? WE'RE TALKING, MORNING, NOON AND NIGHT SICKNESS.

4. THE WORLD BEGINS TO SMELL STRANGE AND YOU THINK YOU COULD FREELANCE WITH POLICE DOGS TO SNIFF OUT ILLEGAL SUBSTANCES.

3. FEEL LIKE YOU'RE LOSING YOUR MIND OR CONTROL OF YOUR EMOTIONS? WELCOME TO PREGNANCY INSANITY.

2. YOU MAY THINK NO PERIOD IS A TELLTALE SIGN, THOUGH FOR YOU IRREGULAR GALS, IT'S OFTEN NOT YOUR FIRST CLUE.

1. WORLD-FAMOUS WOMEN'S INTUITION. MANY WOMEN SWEAR THEY KNEW THE MOMENT OF CONCEPTION.

DATE _____

If it wasn't your doctor who performed your pregnancy test, then today is the day you should call and make an appointment (if you haven't already). Most women can take a dozen home pregnancy tests, line them up on the bathroom counter and read all positive results and still not consider themselves officially pregnant until someone in a surgery with a plastic model of a uterus on display tells them it is so.

NOTES

_____

_____

_____

_____

_____

_____

DATE _____

Almost all men ask the same ridiculous question when their partners announce they are pregnant. 'Are you sure?'

They don't mean to challenge your ability to understand the instructions 'blue, pregnant; white, not pregnant'. It's just that they want you to make it clear for them that they have, indeed, been tagged 'it' and there is no mistake.

Be honest, you felt the same way, too, when you first learned the news.

NotES

_____

_____

_____

_____

_____

_____

DATE _____

So, exactly how long is this going to last? The average pregnancy is anywhere from 240 to 300 days, with most people accepting 280 as the norm. Slightly more women give birth before the full 280 days than after, but only 5 per cent actually deliver the goods on their due date.

Notes

_____
_____
_____
_____
_____
_____

FIRST TRIMESTER 247 DAYS TO GO

DATE _____

Here's a little maths to keep your addled mind in shape. To calculate your due date, count back three months from the first day of your last period, then add seven days to that number. Oh, never mind, ask your midwife to work it out for you.

It's never accurate anyway.

NoteS

_____
_____
_____
_____
_____
_____

DATE _ _ _ _ _ _ _ _ _ _ _ _ _

Prepare to become a 'precious vessel' for the next nine (ten) months.
People just love pregnant women. They will want to protect and
encourage you. They will also want to give you unsolicited advice and
subject you to endless stories about their own pregnancies, or any other
pregnancy they have heard of. Practise smiling and silently make lists of
potential baby names while they prattle on.

NOTES

_____

_____

_____

_____

_____

_____

HOT WATER BOTTLE

DATE _____

It's common to get period pains during the first few weeks of your pregnancy.

It doesn't mean you're getting your period, simply that your uterus is getting adjusted to its new job. Don't worry about the pains if they are fairly mild and not accompanied by bleeding, because they do not signify any danger to the pregnancy. You are fine . . . just another victim of nature's practical jokes.

Notes

_____

_____

_____

_____

_____

_____

DATE _____

Stop torturing yourself because you had a couple of drinks, were on medication or addicted to diet cokes before you realized you were pregnant. If only people who were vice-free had babies, there would be no such thing as rock and roll.

Talk to your doctor* about your concerns . . . doctors are never as scandalized as you think they'll be. The baby will be fine, but do clean up your act now since it's not nice to be selfish.

* You will be under the care of a consultant obstetrician at the hospital in which you plan to have your baby, although in a normal pregnancy you may not see him or her. Your care will probably be shared between your GP and the hospital midwives.

NOTES

_____

_____

_____

_____

TOP 10 GREATEST CONCERNS OF PREGNANT WOMEN

10. WILL MY BREASTS STAY THIS BIG FOREVER? (PLEASE, GOD!)

9. WILL I FEEL THIS SICK AND TIRED FOR THE ENTIRE NINE (TEN) MONTHS?

8. WILL MY PARTNER EVER REALLY UNDERSTAND WHAT I AM GOING THROUGH?

7. WILL IT HURT TO DELIVER THE BABY?

6. HOW BADLY WILL IT HURT TO DELIVER THE BABY?

5. WILL IT HURT MORE THAN A BIKINI WAX? LESS THAN A BROKEN LEG?

4. WILL I GET ALL UGLY AND FAT?

3. WILL EVERYTHING DOWN THERE SHRINK BACK TO NORMAL AFTER THE BABY IS BORN?

2. WILL I BE A GOOD MOTHER?

1. WILL THE BABY BE OK?

DATE _____

Morning sickness does not usually begin its siege the minute you pass the pregnancy test. It lulls you into a false sense of security and then strikes just when you are certain you have avoided nausea completely.

So don't start the self-congratulating yet, because it still might rear its ugly head.

Notes

_____

_____

_____

_____

_____

_____

DATE _____

Isn't it scary how devoted you already feel to this pregnancy? Just a few days ago, you were obliviously living your life, unaware of your little passenger. You might not have even been trying to get pregnant. And now your entire consciousness is devoted to staying pregnant.

They really get a hold on us early.

Notes

_____

_____

_____

_____

_____

_____

DATE _____

Sit down because I have something unbelievable to tell you. Right about now your baby's heart will begin to beat. Think about it . . . there is a little human inside of you! It will be a few more weeks before the doctor can let you hear the heartbeat, but by next week, you can see the heartbeat on an ultrasound. It looks like a kidney bean with a flickering light inside.

NOTES

_____

_____

_____

_____

_____

_____

DATE _____

Feeling a bit haggard, Best Friend? Perhaps it's because your bladder has turned against you. This mutinous organ seems to wake you up every time you settle into a nice dream state. Try to outsmart it . . . don't drink fluids after dinner. This will help a little, but the only real cure is the passage of time. This urgency to pee passes as the progesterone levels out. Trouble is, it comes back again in the third trimester when your bladder is little more than a foetal trampoline.

NOTES

_____

_____

_____

_____

_____

_____

DATE _____

Do you feel addle-brained yet?

A constant state of confusion and distraction defines the mental health of pregnant women. You get so involved with what's going on inside you that, at times, the outside world is little more than an intrusion.

Notes

_____

_____

_____

_____

_____

_____

DATE _____

Rarely do we Best Friends preach, and we generally loathe it when people do it to us.

But here is our one exception.

YOU MUST STOP SMOKING NOW.

It's not just bad for your pregnancy, but we know that if you smoke now, you are almost certain to smoke after the baby is born, and that is akin to raising your child in a tube station, as far as we're concerned. Don't be embarrassed, you probably haven't done any damage to your baby (after all, many of our own mothers smoked when pregnant with us), but you will if this habit persists.

Notes

_____

_____

_____

_____

DATE _____

Spend your lunch hour at a bookshop (preferably one that allows you to eat and browse at the same time). Look at all the books about pregnancy. Then immediately disregard all those written by people who have never given birth. Among the two or three that are left, toss out those that have any scary parts. Now, proceed to the counter and buy *The Best Friends' Guide to Pregnancy*.

NOTES

_____

_____

_____

_____

_____

_____

DATE _____

If you have a private health-care plan, it's never too early to check your policy to see what pregnancy procedures are covered and how long it will pay for you and the baby to recover in the hospital after delivery, if that's what you want. Call and speak to the insurers to clarify anything you don't understand, and then get their names so that you can blame them later. Come to think of it, this is a good job for your partner.

NOTES

_____

_____

_____

_____

_____

_____

DATE _____

Spend some time today ringing Best Friends who have had babies in your area and asking them about their midwives. You may want someone who shares your childbirth vision and understands your particular little needs, such as a willingness to take your call immediately when you can't work out where the hair that is sprouting out of your nipple came from.

NOtes

_____

_____

_____

_____

_____

_____

DATE _____

The best way to find a midwife is the same way we find hairdressers,
plastic surgeons and shops with a sale on; we ask our Best Friends.
Sure, your GP can refer you to someone, but the real skinny comes from
someone who has actually launched a baby and lived to tell about it.

NOTES

_____

_____

_____

_____

_____

_____

FIRST TRIMESTER 233 DAYS TO GO

DATE _____

A major consideration in choosing a midwife is learning about the hospital they recommend, or work in. This can be particularly crucial in cities, where there are several hospitals in which babies are delivered. Does the hospital your potential midwife works in have a neonatal intensive care unit should you need it? What are the birthing rooms like? How far is the drive from your home? Most critical of all, does this hospital have a full-time anaesthetist so you won't be calling out in vain for pain relief at 4 A.M.?

NOTES:

_____

_____

_____

_____

_____

_____

DATE _____

Are you hoping for a boy or a girl? I'm not talking about your baby; I mean your midwife. While there are still significantly more women in this practice, there are men, too. You may just find yourself more comfortable being looked after by someone who was born with a uterus. As one Best Friend asked, 'Would you hire a mechanic who had never even driven a car before?'

NoteS:

DATE _____

Remember, morning sickness is arbitrary, like being picked for jury service. It is no reflection on how well you are doing in this pregnancy.

Notes

_____

_____

_____

_____

_____

_____

DATE _____

If this is your second or subsequent pregnancy, you will notice that you already look pregnant. Those taut little stomach muscles were permanently traumatized by your first pregnancy, and they let go as soon as they got the news about the new baby.

NOTES

_____

_____

_____

_____

_____

_____

DATE _____

No matter how urgent your need to express yourself, try to sound calm when reminding your mate that your luscious new breasts are to be admired from afar for a few more weeks. Men are jumpy as it is, and they get worse after having been slapped a couple of times when they reached for their new 'toys'.

NOTES

_____

_____

_____

_____

_____

_____

TOP 10 COMMANDMENTS OF MORNING SICKNESS

10. EAT SMALL AMOUNTS OF BLAND FOODS ALL DAY LONG.

9. DON'T EAT ANYTHING THAT DOESN'T SMELL APPEALING TO YOU.

8. EAT SOMETHING AROUND 4 A.M., OR AFTER YOUR LAST MIDDLE-OF-THE-NIGHT VISIT TO THE TOILET.

7. TAKE YOUR VITAMIN SUPPLEMENTS – IF PRESCRIBED – AT NIGHT, OR STOP ALTOGETHER UNTIL YOU ARE FEELING BETTER. (YOUR DOCTOR MAY WANT YOU TO TAKE FOLIC ACID SUPPLEMENTS IN THE MEANTIME.)

6. DO NOT TAKE YOUR VITAMINS WITH CITRUS JUICE.

5. WHEN NOTHING SOUNDS APPETIZING, TRY A BOWL OF CEREAL WITH MILK, OR A PIECE OF SWEET FRUIT.

4. IF THE THOUGHT OF CHEWING ANY KIND OF FOOD MAKES YOU SICK, TRY SUCKING ON NATURAL LIQUORICE DROPS.

3. TRY WEARING SEABANDS – THESE ARE SOLD IN CHEMISTS' TO PREVENT SEASICKNESS.

2. SKIP THE DRY BISCUITS UNLESS YOU HAVE A REAL CRAVING FOR THEM (WHICH I CAN'T IMAGINE UNLESS YOU ARE A PARROT).

1. FOLLOW YOUR CRAVINGS. IF YOU REALLY WANT SOME PARTICULAR TYPE OF FOOD, THERE IS A GOOD CHANCE IT WILL ACTUALLY MAKE YOU FEEL A LITTLE BETTER IF YOU EAT IT.

DATE _____

Antenatal vitamins are the size of Scud missiles. I swear I have seen cellular phones that are smaller. If you have trouble swallowing yours without gagging during this trimester of what might seem like constant gagging, try washing them down with something tastier than water. Chocolate milk can be nice; after all, you do need the calcium. Just don't take them with citrus juice since the acid can make them even more offensive to your sensitive stomach.

NOTES

_____

_____

_____

_____

_____

_____

DATE _____

Let's talk about food. The Best Friends' rule of thumb is this: don't eat anything that makes your stomach lurch just because some dumb book says that you should. And don't deny yourself an ice cream cone every now and then, if that's what you have your chubby little heart set on. Moderation in everything, Best Friend, except maybe self-congratulations, which you should be showering on yourself.

Notes

_____

_____

_____

_____

_____

_____

DATE _____

Become friends with the morning chat shows. It really helps to combat
morning sickness if you take fifteen to twenty minutes to get out of bed in
the morning (of course, it helps even more not to get out of bed at all,
but we're dreamin' here). Breakfast in bed is even better, so sweetly
suggest to your partner that a little toast and tea would be tremendously
appreciated.

NOTES

_____

_____

_____

_____

_____

_____

DATE _____

Some men get morning sickness and food cravings to keep their pregnant partners company. Yeah, right! If yours does, firmly remind him that there is only room for one heifer in this corral, pardner.

No Braxton Hicks contractions? No rewards of Rocky Road in a sugar cone.

Notes

_____

_____

_____

_____

_____

_____

DATE _____

Stand up slowly! Many gestating women experience light-headedness and dizziness because pregnancy has lowered their blood pressure. Getting out of bed can be particularly disorienting (isn't it always?), so give yourself plenty of time to work into a standing position. Two or three hours sounds about right, doesn't it?

NOTES

_____

_____

_____

_____

_____

_____

DATE _____

Food cravings are real and should be indulged.

Begin to trust your instincts in this pregnancy/motherhood area, even if you end up eating nectarines four times a day for three weeks straight. It may not be that your body has a natural, infallible nutrition gauge, but it does instinctively know what it can eat without vomiting.

Notes

_____

_____

_____

_____

_____

_____

DATE _____

Naps are completely appropriate during
this time, be they in bed, at your desk, or
on the copier room floor. Just make sure you aren't lying on any
important documents or precious fabrics, because pregnant nappers tend
to drool.

NOTES

DATE _____

Take a closer look in the mirror after your shower this morning. See how brown your nipples look? How about all those blue veins running like road maps over your breasts? Yes, pregnancy is a total body experience.

Notes

_____

_____

_____

_____

_____

_____

DATE _____

Do you have more headaches these days? Let's see, why could that be? Your hormones are at a toxic level, you aren't getting enough sleep, you've gone cold turkey on caffeine and diet coke and you are a little distracted by your impending motherhood. Knock yourself out and take a paracetamol, but remember to ask your doctor first (God, we're conscientious)! If this is your biggest transgression in ten months, you must be a close personal friend of Mother Teresa.

NOTES

_____

_____

_____

_____

_____

_____

DATE _ _ _ _ _ _ _ _ _ _ _ _ _

Are ordinary smells beginning to offend you? Join the club and give the cat feeding and litter tray jobs to your partner. Keep the windows wide open, especially in the car, whenever weather permits. It's also a good idea to stay out of all delicatessens and the dairy section of your supermarket. Don't trust your nose implicitly, however. Always get a second opinion from a non-gestater before throwing an entire meat loaf down the waste disposal.

NOtes

_ _

_ _

_ _

_ _

_ _

_ _

DATE ---------------

Having a hard time eating foods from all the major food groups? Don't fret . . . many pregnant women can live on little more than toasted cheese sandwiches on white bread for days on end. Go easy on yourself and avoid all foods that make your eyes water; you and the baby will still thrive. You'll make up for it in a couple of weeks.

NOTES

DATE --------------

You will be up anyway at 4 or 5 A.M. going to the toilet so take an extra minute to eat a bowl of cereal or a piece of bread before you go back to sleep. A full stomach when you wake up to begin your day can minimize rise-and-shine retching.

NOTES

DATE _____

Treat yourself to one of those books that show photos of babies as they grow in the uterus. Skip any of the scary or preachy text, but find the pictures because they are miraculous. I still can't work out how they got the camera in there!

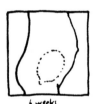 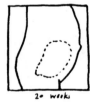 

6 weeks   20 weeks   28 weeks

NOTES

_____

_____

_____

_____

_____

_____

DATE _____

Want to change your mind about the motherhood business? On second thought, does this 280 days of growing big as a hippo (an adorable hippo, of course) and delivering a baby out of your dainty little privates appal more than thrill you? Every honest Best Friend will admit to times of wanting to escape her pregnancy. Don't worry, this is just a sign of your superior intelligence in considering the full nature of the task you have undertaken.

Notes

_____

_____

_____

_____

_____

_____

DATE _____

Now that you are pregnant, do you find that you adore all babies? If the answer is no, don't worry your pretty little head one minute. I can say, with total certainty, that your own little baby will be much prettier, quieter, cleaner and generally superior to the garden-variety babies you see in public. I know mine were.

NOTES

_____

_____

_____

_____

_____

_____

DATE _____

Guess what . . . your partner is pregnant, too! And he may be having a hard time digesting the fact that, even though he has the emotional inner life of a fifteen-year-old, he is turning into Robbie Coltrane. Don't be surprised if he takes on some of your pregnancy symptoms. If you sleep a lot, he may, too. If you crave raspberry sorbet, he may, too. If you feel nauseous, he may, too. Try to be tolerant, but feel free to draw the line if he also gets wind.

NOTES

_____

_____

_____

_____

_____

_____

DATE _____

Not feeling like your usual sexy self? What with nausea, sore breasts and fatigue, most 'breeders' like you couldn't care less about shaving their legs and slipping on the black stockings. In fact, getting your teeth brushed might be the most attention you have paid to your appearance for days. Don't worry, Best Friend. Rent your partner a sexy video (you can nap during it) and wait a few more weeks because the second trimester just may unleash the sex goddess in you.

NOTES

_____

_____

_____

_____

_____

_____

TOP 10 FEARS OF PARTNERS OF PREGNANT WOMEN

10. HE WILL BE FORCED TO CUT THE UMBILICAL CORD.

9. HE WILL FAINT DURING DELIVERY (OR WORSE YET, HE WILL STAY CONSCIOUS AND HAVE TO WATCH THE WHOLE THING).

8. HE WILL NEVER BE ABLE TO HAVE SEX WITH YOU AGAIN AFTER SEEING HIS FAVOURITE PLAYGROUND BULLDOZED BY A BABY'S GIGANTIC HEAD.

7. HE WILL BE AS BAD/GOOD A FATHER AS HIS OWN FATHER WAS.

6. HE WILL BE BOUND TO YOU, A WEEPY, JUMPY, WINDY, OVERWEIGHT SHADOW OF HIS FORMER SWEETHEART, FOR THE REST OF HIS LIFE.

5. HE WILL HAVE TO DELIVER THE BABY HIMSELF.

4. HE WILL NOT BE ABLE TO AFFORD THE BABY (HE MAY HAVE A POINT HERE, BUT DON'T ENCOURAGE HIM.)

3. YOU WILL DIE OR RUN OFF AND LEAVE HIM WITH A TINY STRANGER TO CARE FOR.

2. HE WILL THROW UP DURING DELIVERY AND YOU'LL REPEAT THE TALE FOR THE NEXT TWENTY-FIVE YEARS.

1. IF HE BECOMES A FATHER, HE CANNOT BE THE BABY ANY MORE.

DATE _____

It is very common for fathers-to-be to feel frightened to have sex with their pregnant partners. Apparently, they worry that they will hurt the baby. Isn't it just like a man to automatically overestimate the penetrative powers of his penis? It's up to you how you handle this. If you're feeling amorous, explain that the baby is completely protected. If you crave celibacy, congratulate him on his 'huge' sacrifice.

NOTES

_____

_____

_____

_____

_____

_____

DATE _____

Have you told your father that you're going to have a baby? Think about it
. . . this is the first time the two of you have actually acknowledged that
you are no longer a virgin. If this feels a little bit weird, just wait until you
pull out a giant breast and start breastfeeding in front of him.

Close Encounters of the Freudian Kind.

Notes

_____

_____

_____

_____

_____

_____

DATE _____

You may have been prescribed vitamin supplements. Do us all a favour and don't start adding other vitamin or mineral supplements on the eager-beaver theory that if a little is good, a lot is better. The same logic that has you giving up caffeine and aspirin applies to all that stuff on the shelves in the health food store, too . . . no matter what your sister's yoga teacher says.

NOTES

DATE _____

Most mummy Best Friends have the compassion not to repeat labour and delivery horror stories to pregnancy virgins (hey, good oxymoron!). They wait until you have stories of your own before going into contraction-by-contraction detail of their ordeals.

If someone just can't bear to wait to share tales of endless labours and stitches from stem to stern, you are completely within your rights to stop her. Kindly explain that you want to be 'surprised.'

Notes

_____

_____

_____

_____

_____

_____

DATE _____

Talk about understatement! Most pregnancy books warn that you may experience some 'moodiness' at this special time. Moody, schmoody. Welcome to the madhouse!

Have you found yourself screeching because your partner brought you vanilla ice cream when you clearly asked for chocolate, which only goes to prove that he never listens to you since you clearly said chocolate, and if he ever paid attention he would know by now that you never eat vanilla . . . in fact, you loathe vanilla . . . and if he doesn't care enough about the baby . . .

Never mind, hand over the ice cream!

NOTES

_____

_____

_____

_____

_____

DATE _____

Trousers won't button all the way to the top?

Well, you know what they say, the waistline is the first thing to go.

Here's a trick; take a hair elastic, hook it around the top button, run it through the opposing hole, and then back around the button. There, isn't that a little more comfortable? No one knows but us, and we'll never tell. A perfect time to acknowledge you should no longer be tucking in tops.

Notes

_____

_____

_____

_____

_____

_____

DATE _____

While I have never believed the PMS insanity defence, I must confess that I can see its value for pregnant women. Between memory lapse, distorted judgement and unbearable sensitivity, we can make Sybil look composed.

Suffice it to say, this is not the best time to sign any binding legal documents, operate heavy machinery or change your hairstyle.

NOTES:

_____

_____

_____

_____

_____

_____

DATE _____

Keep big old towels in the front seat of your
car so that you have something to throw up into
if the urge should strike while you are stuck in traffic. One of the most
charming aspects of morning sickness is its refusal to limit itself to those
hours before noon or to respect simulated leather interiors.

Notes:

_____

_____

_____

_____

_____

_____

DATE _____

Don't be afraid to ask your doctor or midwife the questions that really concern you, no matter how ridiculous. Health-care professionals forget how truly uninformed first-timers really are. Remember, no matter how often you may think about your doctor or midwife, he or she only thinks about you while you are sitting (or lying) right in their faces.

No matter how compelling we find ourselves, professionals don't waste their time telling others about the new stooge in their practice.

NOTES

_____
_____
_____
_____
_____
_____

DATE --------------

Don't take it personally if your partner seems less enthusiastic about your pregnancy than you. His breasts don't hurt, he's not worried about

getting the baby out of his body and he certainly isn't crying every time he sees a nappy commercial on TV. It's just not real to him yet.

It turns out that there is absolutely no correlation between a man who is enchanted by his partner's pregnancy and a man who will eventually sacrifice every Saturday morning coaching five-a-side football.

NOTES

DATE _____

Try sucking on liquorice drops to soothe a
choppy stomach. If you hate liquorice, try other boiled sweets. Fruit-
flavoured lollies can do wonders, too. Sure, you are completely ignoring
the champion foods like broccoli, but what's the use of going to the effort
of chewing them if you're just going to throw them up straightaway?

NOTES

_____

_____

_____

_____

_____

_____

DATE _ _ _ _ _ _ _ _ _ _ _ _ _

No pregnancy is fully experienced without the mummy dissolving into tears for no reason at least three or four times. It can be the sound of a lullaby, the sight of your own baby pictures when your own parents looked so young and optimistic or it might be an imagined slight such as no one offering you a seat on the bus. Once the floodgates are open, they are difficult to close again. You might start out crying about one thing . . . then continue to cry about something completely unrelated.

Lie down and apply cool compresses.

Notes

_ _

_ _

_ _

_ _

_ _

_ _

DATE --------------

Meet a new pregnant woman today. Pregnancy is so much more fun when you share it with someone who completely relates to your concerns and shares your obsession with all things baby.

Expectant mums are easy to meet because you already have so much in common. Talk to other women at the clinic or the supermarket. A good icebreaker is, 'So, when are you due?'

After that, they will have to prize you apart.

NOTES

DATE _____

Have you begun fretting about how much or how little (less likely, but it happens) weight you have gained? This is a universal thorn in the ample sides of pregnant women.

Stop comparing yourself to standards in unenlightened books . . . or, worse, soap opera stars, who swear they work up to their due dates and give birth in their dressing rooms during lunch break. It's all fiction or the sign of a personality disorder.

Eat sensibly, take your vitamins and put your scales in the garage.

Notes

_____

_____

_____

_____

_____

_____

Surrender

DATE _____

Surrender, Dorothy! Your body is yours in name only, because a baby has moved in and taken control. And why shouldn't it assume control, since your baby knows at least as much about pregnancy as you do?

Children have a way of laying claim to a mother's body from the time they live in it until the day they steal the car keys.

Notes

_____

_____

_____

_____

_____

_____

DATE _____

As your pregnancy progresses, it will astonish you how much more time
you spend thinking about your baby than your partner does. He can
spend all day without finding a single moment to obsess about baby
names or the fact that caesarean rates are at an all-time high. So, when
you have called him at work for the tenth time today, don't be ashamed;
just think of it as 'sharing'.

Notes

TOP **10** REASONS NOT TO EXERCISE

10. YOU WILL GET FATTER ANYWAY.

9. EXERCISING WILL NOT MAKE LABOUR AND DELIVERY EASIER, SINCE CONTRACTIONS ARE INVOLUNTARY MOVEMENTS OF THE UTERUS, AND THE UTERUS IS A DIFFICULT MUSCLE TO TRAIN IN A GYM.

8. GRAVITY IS HARD ENOUGH ON YOUR VOLUPTUOUS BREASTS AND BUM WHEN YOU'RE STANDING STILL, LET ALONE WHEN YOU'RE HOPPING UP AND DOWN IN A STEP AEROBICS CLASS.

7. IT'S NOT GOOD FOR THE BABY OR YOU TO GET OVERHEATED; IT STARTS TO FEEL LIKE A HARD-BOILED EGG.

6. YOUR LIGAMENTS ARE LOOSER, AND YOU CAN TWIST YOUR KNEES OR ANKLES WITH ONE WOBBLY MOVEMENT.

5. YOUR BODY IS WORKING FULL-TILT MANUFACTURING A HUMAN BEING; DON'T DISTRACT IT WITH LOW-IMPACT-CARDIO-FUNK-'N'-FREE-WEIGHTS CLASSES.

4. YOU MIGHT ENDANGER THE PREGNANCY. EVEN IF YOU DON'T, IF A PROBLEM APPEARS AT ANY TIME DURING PREGNANCY, YOU WILL ALWAYS WONDER IF IT WAS THAT SQUAT MACHINE THAT CAUSED IT.

3. OUR COMPULSION TO EXERCISE WHEN WE ARE PREGNANT IS A REFLECTION OF OUR INABILITY TO SURRENDER AND LET NATURE RUN ITS COURSE. LET THE SUBSCRIPTIONS TO YOUR FASHION MAGAZINES LAPSE TILL FURTHER NOTICE.

2. YOU ARE TOO TIRED.

1. DO YOU REALLY NEED AN EXCUSE?

DATE _____

You should be so proud of yourself. Being pregnant is one of the few
professions that you can be sure you are uniquely qualified for. No
doubts about whether this job is 'creative' enough for you or allows you to
'make a difference'. It's just what Mother Nature had in mind for you,
even if the pay sucks and the hours are definitely a union violation.

Notes

_____

_____

_____

_____

_____

_____

DATE _____

Since there is no graceful way to ask this, I will just plunge in. Are you noticing that you are more lubricated than you were before you were 'with child'? An increase in vaginal discharge is normal. You might want to try panty liners; and even if you are a pants-free gal when you're not pregnant, you *must* wear cotton pants when you are.

NOTES

_____

_____

_____

_____

_____

_____

DATE _____

Thrush is so common in pregnant women you'd think they were bread-makers. If you notice the telltale discomfort, DO NOT TRY TO TREAT IT YOURSELF. In fact, the rule of thumb during pregnancy is never let anything up near your cervix except your partner or your doctor or midwife. Get a prescription cream that is safe for you and the baby.

NOTES

DATE _____

Time to clean out your drawers. All belts and wonderbras can be put into storage until further notice. Never, ever, put a belt around a body without a distinguishable waistline or you will look like a beach umbrella closed up around a football.

Notes

_____

_____

_____

_____

_____

_____

DATE _____

Gazing longingly into the windows of maternity shops, admiring the fashions?

Actually, this is your way of dipping one more toe in the sea of surrender.

If you fight this pregnancy stuff too hard, you really waste a lot of energy.

Make friends with the things that frighten you, like gussets in your pants and knickers big enough to use as pillowcases, because they will definitely be part of your life.

Notes

_____

_____

_____

_____

_____

_____

DATE _____

Try some fresh fruit. Watermelon, nectarines, grapes and apple slices (without the peel) can taste great and stay down in your nauseous tummy.

Experiment, but our Best Friends' advice is to stick to foods that are high in water content so that you don't have to gag to get them down.

Notes

_____

_____

_____

_____

_____

_____

DATE _____

Pregnant women are hot, and I mean that in its most literal sense. Many men complain that their partners keep the house so cold that their breath frosts and that they must hang their heads out of the car window like the family dog. We can't help it . . . we are incubators in the purest sense of the word.

NOTES

DATE _____

Feel like you are coming down with a cold? You might just be coming down with pregnancy chronic stuffy mummy nose. Don't worry, it will clear up in 188 more days.

NOTES

_____

_____

_____

_____

_____

_____

DATE _____

Congratulations on being a walking inspiration of goodwill and boundless optimism (no matter how green and crazy you feel). Since the beginning of time, any woman who has become pregnant by a man who has a job and is not married to someone else has been cheered as if she invented the condition.

At least the first time around.

NOTES

_____

_____

_____

_____

_____

_____

DATE _____

Not a big fan of milk? Worried that since you can't gag down the half litre recommended by greater authorities, you're depriving your baby of the calcium it needs? First of all, if you're shortchanging anyone, it's probably you because the baby gets first shot at your resources. Second of all, this situation can be easily handled by asking your GP to suggest a calcium supplement. Remember, yogurt, cheese and breakfast cereals (if dunked in milk, of course!) all contain calcium.

Notes

_____

_____

_____

_____

_____

_____

DATE _____

When you had your first antenatal visit, you probably received a stack of papers about the miracle of birth. You may have read them or thrown them in the bin, but make sure you know the number to ring, how to get into hospital at night, and what you should bring with you.

NOTES

DATE _____

You may be wondering right about now, 'If the baby is growing in my belly, why is my bum so big?'

The answer lies somewhere in Darwin's theory of evolution: when we still walked on all fours, that bubble bum provided a rumble seat for our babies. Keep this in mind when getting dressed; you should never leave the house without looking in a mirror to check out your backside.

NOTES

DATE _____

Wear something figure-revealing today. Show off your spectacular bustline before your tummy starts competing with it.

Remember, the day will come when the boobs actually sit on the belly AND look small by comparison.

Notes

_____

_____

_____

_____

_____

_____

DATE _____

Always keep water and food in your car. Not
in case of a natural disaster, but because
pregnant means always having to say you're hungry or thirsty.

If you haven't planned ahead and stocked up with water, juice, trail mix
or crackers, you will be forced to pull into fast-food restaurants and
before you know it, you'll have a Quarter-Pounder in each hand.

NOTES

_____

_____

_____

_____

_____

_____

DATE --------------

The 'wind gremlins' should be invading your body any time now, if they aren't already permanent residents. Slower digestion can make you as fragrant as a barnyard animal. Just remember to say 'excuse me' to anyone who has the bad taste to notice, and when it happens at night, do your partner a favour and fluff the sheets.

NOTES

SECOND TRIMESTER   180 DAYS TO GO

DATE   _____

Do you wake up feeling svelte and light in the mornings and then get
fatter and heavier as the day goes on? Most expectant women can't wait
until the end of the day, when they can pull off their shoes, yank off the
support tights and ease out of the trousers that have been unzipped
since lunchtime. At the top of the pleasure heap is taking off your bra
and having a good tummy scratch.

Notes

_____

_____

_____

_____

_____

_____

DATE _____

Let's talk about pets for a moment. Are you crazy about your kitty? That's all well and good, but you shouldn't be touching any dirty cat litter because it carries critters that are dangerous to pregnant women. How about your dog that has been like a child to you all these years? Trust us when we tell you that it will rejoin the animal world once your real baby comes. One last note . . . if you have lizards, snakes or other reptiles, talk to several paediatricians (and a psychiatrist or two). Many doctors think that those pets carry infections that are very dangerous to babies and young children.

Notes

_____

_____

_____

_____

_____

_____

DATE _____

Every time you ask yourself, 'Can I go one more day without having to wash my hair?' shout 'No!' You have more hair now that you're pregnant, and it gets heavy and dull faster now. Make the extra effort because a good hair day can compensate for a bad complexion day.

Notes

_____

_____

_____

_____

_____

_____

DATE _____

You should be getting an ultrasound soon to see what your little darling looks like, inside and out. You will be advised to fill your bladder to enhance the picture, and we're not talking a little bit filled. Just wait until you've gulped down three 500 ml glasses of water and are forbidden to pee. Does the term 'Chinese water torture' suddenly seem more meaningful to you?

Notes

_____

_____

_____

_____

_____

_____

Boy? girl?

DATE _____

Boy or girl? Do you and your partner want to know ahead of time? An ultrasound as early as now could give you that information if you want it. If you don't, make sure to tell every single person you encounter on your way to the ultrasound appointment, from the parking attendant, to the receptionist, to the technicians, to the doctor (who may have forgotten since you last discussed this). People often can't conceal their excitement when they spot a little penis on the screen (or the absence thereof), and they immediately start calling it 'he' or 'she'.

Notes

_____

_____

_____

_____

_____

_____

SECOND TRIMESTER 175 DAYS TO GO

DATE _____

Remember: your pregnancy is not your mother's pregnancy. She probably smoked and drank and kept her coffee habit when she was pregnant with you, she was asleep when you were born and she recuperated in the hospital for a week or two afterwards. So, if she starts telling you that you're neurotic about microwaves and NutraSweet, or that you're getting far too fat, ignore her.

NOTES

_____

_____

_____

_____

_____

_____

DATE _____

Starting today, you should begin
phasing out any clothing with
padded shoulders from your
wardrobe. I know maternity shops are chock-full of shoulder pads,
probably on the fashion assumption that the bigger your shoulders look,
the smaller your bum and belly will look. Don't use them, Best Friend . . .
you would need shoulders like John Wayne's to minimize your tummy by
the end of this trimester. Shoulder pads make your arms and neck look
even fatter than they actually are.

NOTES

_____

_____

_____

_____

_____

_____

DATE _____

To paraphrase a common car-safety warning, 'Caution: objects in mirror are fatter than they appear.' You have been living in this growing, changing body for several months now, and you may have actually become accustomed to how you look. While this is a sign of a healthy state of mind, it can prove disastrous in fashion. It is very likely that you have outgrown many of the clothes you are still wearing. Take a closer look . . . it might be time for a maternity shop visit.

Notes

_____

_____

_____

_____

_____

_____

DATE _____

Doesn't food taste fabulous these days? You wolf down with enthusiasm even 'good for you' stuff like salads. You know how we Best Friends feel about watching our weight during pregnancy – deeply offended – so we are nothing but happy for you and your local frozen yogurt parlour.

One word of caution, however: many men get cranky if you eat the food off their plates after you have hoovered your own. No matter how good those french fries look sitting before him, keep your hands off.

Notes

_____

_____

_____

_____

_____

_____

DATE _____

How's your skin doing? If you have been battling pimples, you might be finding that your skin is clearer. On the other hand, you may start to notice patches of darker skin across your nose and cheeks. This is called *chloasma*, but it is more sinisterly known as the 'mask of pregnancy' (as if it provided any kind of disguise whatsoever!). This is just another pregnancy thing, and there isn't much you can do about it, except wear sunblock even when the only light you see comes from inside the fridge.

Notes

_____

_____

_____

_____

_____

_____

DATE _____

Are you taking iron supplements along with or in your antenatal vitamins? If you are, this iron might be contributing to the constipation that plagues most pregnant women. It is also to blame for the unfamiliarly dark stools you may have noticed. I used to think it looked like tyre rubber, myself.

Ask your doctor if you can take a break from iron for a while, or if a stool softener could be your salvation.

Notes

_____

_____

_____

_____

_____

_____

DATE _____

Amniocentesis (am-nee-oh-cen-TEE-sis) is traditionally performed around the sixteenth week of pregnancy in women who are over the age of thirty-five (or thirty-six, or thirty-eight, depending on where you live) or who have a history of genetic problems.

It is done by drawing amniotic fluid out through a very long needle in your belly. Does this hurt? Surprisingly, no. Is it creepy?

Yes, so bring someone into the room with you to distract you with droll conversation and discuss the images on the ultrasound monitor with you . . . 'Is that a leg or a penis?'

Notes

_____

_____

_____

_____

DATE _____

Stay in bed the day of and the day after your amnio. Sure, you probably feel fine, just exhausted by the small nervous breakdown you had before the procedure, but you must rest anyway. You have just sprung a small leak, and only a person who thinks pregnancy is something to be overcome, rather than accepted, would even consider leaping up to go back to the office or stock up on a few things from Tesco.

Besides, once the baby is born, you will never be allowed to lie in bed to recuperate from anything short of open-heart surgery.

Notes

_____

_____

_____

_____

_____

_____

DATE _____

It usually takes up to three weeks to get the results of your amniocentesis
. . . easily the longest three weeks of your existence. There isn't really
much we can suggest to help you endure this trial; just stay as busy as
you can, and remember how overwhelmingly in your favour the odds of
perfection really are.

Don't fool yourself into thinking that the good results from your amnio will
leave you worry-free for the rest of your pregnancy. Your fertile mind will
move right on to unsightly birthmarks, hearing difficulties, even the big
nose you once had. Remember, nothing can live up to your vivid
imagination.

NOTES

_____

_____

_____

_____

_____

DATE -------------

Here's the news: the only way to prevent stretch marks is to pick your mother carefully. You see, a propensity toward those maligned marks is genetic. You can massage gallons of potions, lotions and health food store oils into your skin, and you will still get stretch marks if that's what nature had in mind for you.

The general rule is: oil massages don't prevent stretch marks, they create pregnancies.

Notes

DATE _____

This time of pregnancy often brings such a sense of well-being and vigour that you might feel even more terrific than you do when you're not pregnant. Lots of Best Friends report that their immunity to colds and flus is stronger, their energy is boundless and they feel sexy and aroused. Of course, this could be an exaggerated response to the relief they feel at not being sick and tired like they were in the first trimester. Either way, if you are feeling exceptionally well, live it up because you may not feel this great again till your next pregnancy.

NOTES

_____

_____

_____

_____

_____

_____

DATE _____

Now that you are feeling better, it's time to consider your pregnancy

exercise routine. Our suggestion is elegant in its simplicity and ease: give

up all exercise classes, free weights, climbers and thigh-masters. Swim if

you must, or take a walk now and then, but don't buy into that

brainwashing that says exercising will help prepare you for labour and

delivery, unless Nautilus has invented a uterus machine since my last

visit to the gym.

Notes

_____

_____

_____

_____

_____

_____

DATE _____

By virtue of being a non-female, your partner will have absolutely no idea what it feels like to be in your shoes. He will not truly know your anxiety, your ambivalence, your insecurities or your near-toxic hormonal state. That's enough right there to qualify him for the title of World's Most Annoying Man.

All we can offer is the assurance that he's no worse than most, and he will look a lot better with his baby in his arms.

NOTES

_____
_____
_____
_____
_____
_____

DATE _____

Sex is beginning to look a lot more interesting, isn't it? First of all, you are probably coming off a long, dry spell, what with all that nausea, fatigue and atomic tits. Second, your pregnancy hormones are settling into a nice little aphrodisiac cocktail. And it can't hurt that your 'privates' are chronically engorged with blood, a state they used to be able to achieve only through foreplay. Your body is your sex toy and your partner your slave. Have fun while it lasts!

Notes

_____

_____

_____

_____

_____

_____

DATE _____

The Best Friends recommend the top position for pregnant sex. This allows you to present your breasts in a tantalizing way and keep your lumpy rear end where it belongs . . . out of sight.

Best of all, this position gives you control over how deep the penetration goes . . . and really, control is everything, isn't it?

NOTES

_____

_____

_____

_____

_____

_____

DATE _____

Lots of Best Friends have very sexy dreams during this part of pregnancy. Not just sexy, like, say, a Barbara Cartland novel.

No, we're talking Pussycat Theatre stuff, all in your own little imagination.

When you wake after one of these doozies, it won't be to make yet another trip to the bathroom, but to attack your unsuspecting partner for a reenactment.

Notes

_____
_____
_____
_____
_____
_____

DATE _____

For Best Friends experiencing a sexual renaissance, the general rules of thumb are:

1. Quick to arouse (in fact, some say in constant state of arousal).

2. Slower to climax.

3. And when you do climax, it is like a 9.0 on the Richter scale, with several aftershocks, courtesy of Mother (of course) Nature.

NOTES

DATE   _____

There isn't much in the way of sexy maternity lingerie, but you are probably still small enough to wear larger sizes of real people's lingerie. The idea is to emphasize the breasts and conceal the hips and bum. Think empire waists or a bra and pants peeking out of a robe or kimono. By the time the robe comes off, odds are good that the lights will be off or the covers can be artfully arranged over your fanny.

Notes

_____

_____

_____

_____

_____

_____

DATE --------------

Sex, if you're indeed having sex, gets more physically challenging in your fifth and sixth months of pregnancy. Even if your belly does not protrude enough to create a barricade between you and your partner, it is probably heavy enough to make you feel like fainting when you lie flat on your back.

For heaven's sake, don't let this stop you!

Try some position other than missionary. One Best Friend's favourite is called 'spoons', and it involves the two of you lying on your sides, facing in the same direction, with your fella behind you. Any 'rear' approach will work, but many women think that 'doggy style' hurts because of that deeper penetration.

NOTES

DATE _____

If you are, indeed, feeling more like your old self, don't share that information with your partner. He will feel so relieved that his 'real' lady has come back that he will be less concerned about you and begin to take you for granted.

Men can forget they are pregnant for hours on end, and it is our job to keep that from happening.

Don't ever let him labour under the delusion that gestating is part-time work.

NOTES

_____

_____

_____

_____

_____

_____

DATE _____

It is not considered bad form to use your pregnancy as an excuse or
special circumstance, but if you don't look undeniably pregnant yet, you
must speak up and state your needs. You might consider trying it out on
public transport (unless, of course, you live in London), on a police
officer who has stopped you for speeding ('My blood sugar was dropping
and I needed to hurry to the nearest fast-food restaurant!') or in a snooty
boutique that refuses to share its loo. It goes without saying that you
should use it on your partner any time you want since he won't fall for it
for any pregnancy after this one.

NOTES

DATE _____

Oops! Just when you thought you had this pregnancy thing licked, you have another bout of nausea and uncontrollable emotions. As Kermit the Frog sings, 'It's not easy being green.'

NOTES

_____

_____

_____

_____

_____

_____

DATE _____

There's an old maxim about pregnancy that says, 'A tooth for every baby.' In generations past, mums-to-be just expected to have serious dental problems added to the list of maternity trials and tribulations.

In every cliché, there is a nugget of truth, and the truth about this one is that pregnant women must pay particular attention to their teeth, and perhaps more specifically, their gums. You may notice your gums bleed easily when you brush them. This can lead to infection and decay if you don't consult your dentist at least twice during pregnancy and follow his or her orders.

Notes

_____

_____

_____

_____

_____

_____

DATE _ _ _ _ _ _ _ _ _ _ _ _ _

Take a good look at your legs in a three-way mirror before leaving the house in pedal-pushers or a miniskirt. Some long-limbed pregnant Best Friends can show off their legs all summer long, but those of us who are described in fashion magazines as 'pear-shaped' tend to get enough cellulite to make our thighs look like relief maps of Switzerland.

Notes

_____

_____

_____

_____

_____

_____

DATE _____

This is generally about the time when people start talking to you about what you might like 'for the baby'. These gifts are great and are to be encouraged since no one can really afford all the baby paraphernalia you think you'll need.

Our advice is: wait and weigh all offers until about the sixth month and draw up and circulate a list.

Notes

DATE _____

This pregnancy business isn't half bad, is it? In fact, you might begin to wonder at this point what all those other pregnant women have been moaning and complaining about.

You can carry this off . . . no problem.

Lots of energy, not too fat. Secure in your ability to become a mother, you feel like a million dollars, right? Hey, it's us you're talking to, Friend, get real!

Notes

DATE _____

Even though the common prohibition against pregnant women stewing in saunas and jacuzzis makes good sense, your own friendly home bathtub can be your best friend right up until your waters break or you lose your mucous plug.

The critical difference between your bath and the health club jacuzzi, leaving out for the moment our morbid fear of the bacteria of strangers, is that the jacuzzi does not cool off and your bath does. It's that exposure to unrelenting heat that can dangerously raise your core body temperature.

NOTES

_____
_____
_____
_____
_____
_____

DATE _____

Until they know and adore them personally, most men tend to think of babies as shortcuts to the poorhouse. They know how much food kids eat (especially teenagers), they assume a new home is looming in their future, and anyone who has read *Time* magazine knows that college in eighteen years will cost more than that looming new home. All this worrying is good; it distracts them and makes the pregnancy pass more quickly.

Notes

_____

_____

_____

_____

_____

_____

DATE _____

Pregnancy is as good a time as any to settle your issues with your own mother. You may have your mother's chin or her laugh or her bum, but you are not your mother.

Here's your chance to appraise your own childhood and pick and choose the parts you want to share with your kids and the parts you want to spare them.

NoteS

_____

_____

_____

_____

_____

_____

DATE _____

Lots of pregnant women have a secret fear that they will be a bad mother. Either their own mother was so extraordinarily loving, patient and selfless that they know they could never, in a million years, be as good as she was . . . or their mother was such a selfish, neglectful and undemonstrative person that they are terrified they may be genetically predisposed to act just like her. Take heart, your baby will think you're perfect for at least ten or eleven years.

Notes

_____

_____

_____

_____

_____

_____

DATE _____

There is no predicting what your pregnancy will be like, just as there is no deep instinctual knowledge about giving birth or breastfeeding a baby. Just make it up as you go along; everybody else does.

NOTES

_____

_____

_____

_____

_____

_____

DATE _____

Some women take this pregnancy purity business a tad too far. Sure, we are unanimous in the righteousness of giving up smoking and drug use and we are fairly unanimous about not drinking alcohol. We start splitting ranks over microwaved food, airport security, coffee and sugar. And we have had it up to here with women who freak out about chemicals in cot mattresses and the use of dental anaesthetics. The idea is to be protective, not paranoid.

NOTES

_____

_____

_____

_____

_____

_____

DATE _____

Lots of women in your shoes (which, by the way, must be feeling a bit tight) are frustrated that they don't look pregnant enough to look . . . well, pregnant. Your friends who have children already will smile wickedly and say 'Just wait . . .'. But you can't believe that you are already five months pregnant and you don't look ripe with child.

First of all, let me remind you that pregnancy is a ten-month affair, so you still have plenty of time for expansion. I promise you that you will not reach the end of the pregnancy feeling gypped that you didn't get big enough.

NOTES

_____

_____

_____

_____

_____

_____

DATE _____

Can you feel the baby moving yet? Maybe you think you have been feeling it for a couple of weeks, but have just now become certain that it's the baby and not wind. Either way, feeling the presence of your child is out of this world.

The Best Friends agree that, of all the experiences of pregnancy, feeling the baby move is the one we miss the most (or, in some cases, the only thing we miss). It's like having a wonderful secret; you feel kind of smug, like when you're the only one at a party who knows that you aren't wearing underwear.

Notes

Kerri

Dawn

Don

DATE --------------

Rarely are men and women unanimous about anything from whether to share the Caesar salad for two in a restaurant to what show to watch on television. Why on earth would you expect to agree on the baby's name?

Actually, the ideal time to lobby for *your* favourite name is during labour, when your partner is terrified and will do anything to comfort you.

Jack

Alvin

NOtes

Lucy

Paul

DATE _____

Mae

We mums obsess over baby names.

So why is it your partner seems so unconcerned with this baby-naming business?

What does he think . . . that they hand out names at the hospital?

James

Eloise

NOTES

_____

_____

_____

_____

_____

_____

DATE _____

If you are exceptions to the rule and you and your partner have settled on
a name for the baby, don't tell it to anyone, no matter how they beg!
People feel completely free to challenge your selection at any time before
the moniker is typed on to the birth certificate. Your beloved name will
inevitably be the same as that of the little girl in your brother-in-law's
second-grade class who picked her nose and ate it.

After the baby and its name have bonded, no one will dare say anything
unflattering about your choice, no matter how bad it is.

NOTES

_____

_____

_____

_____

_____

_____

DATE _____

Some books, especially those written by people who have never been pregnant, describe the sensation of the baby moving within you as wind. This is not very accurate. It feels like there is a feather or a cottonball stroking or tapping you on the inside. It can also be a lurching sensation, like when you are startled. Think roller coaster on flat land.

Notes

_____

_____

_____

_____

_____

_____

DATE _____

Braxton Hicks contractions are contractions of the uterus during pregnancy that *do not* open up your cervix. Later, you may be told you are having 'false labour' when your abdomen gets hard enough to bounce pennies off it, but there is nothing false about them. They are, in fact, good preparation for labour. The good news is that they don't really hurt, but they really can grab your attention.

NOTES

DATE _ _ _ _ _ _ _ _ _ _ _ _ _

Be brave. It is time for your first visit to a maternity shop as a real customer. I know, your belly doesn't stick *that* far out yet, but at the rate you're growing, you won't realize you're a candidate for elastic-waist trousers with a panel until you are half-dressed and crying in your bedroom because you can't find anything that fits.

Notes

_____

_____

_____

_____

_____

_____

DATE _____

Lots of otherwise intelligent people maintain that you can make your baby smarter and more closely bonded with you if you and your partner speak to it in your tummy. Our guess is that babies' grasp of English is still minimal, so they don't really know which of our many conversations throughout the day are directed at them. That means you are probably meeting your New Age maternal obligations simply by letting the little foetus eavesdrop on your telephone conversations.

One thing does seem certain: your newborn will recognize your voice and quiet down to hear it, even in the delivery room.

NOTES

_____

_____

_____

_____

_____

_____

DATE _____

Some women notice an increase in their saliva production, of all unnecessary functions, when they are pregnant.

Carry a supply of boiled sweets to keep up the sucking action, and tissues to catch any spillover. Otherwise, you will end up talking like Tweety's friend, Sylvester: 'Ssssufferin' ssssuccotash!'

NOTES

_____

_____

_____

_____

_____

_____

DATE _____

Are you a little nervous about discussing maternity
leave with your boss? Or are you even more nervous
because you don't really know if you plan to go back
to work at all after the baby is born? Trust our
combined Best Friends' experience when we say

that the way the system works, you pretty much have to say you are
returning to work immediately after your maternity leave, no matter what
your real plans are. That means that you will receive your statutory
maternity pay, but anything other than that is usually stated in your
contract of employment or negotiated.

NOTES

_____

_____

_____

_____

_____

DATE _____

It is now time to learn
to sleep on your
side, your left

side in particular. You already probably feel weird sleeping on your
tummy for fear of squashing anybody, but your back is becoming
inappropriate now, too. Even before you can feel the effects, the baby is
getting heavy enough to put a kink in the main artery that runs from your
heart down into your legs, much like when a car tyre runs over the
garden hose. It will take you a while to adapt to this single sleep option,
but fatigue always overcomes a little discomfort.

Notes

_____
_____
_____
_____
_____

DATE _____

This is the time to get reacquainted with your pillows. They will no longer be mere pieces of furniture, but rather dear and valued friends.

And, as we all know, you can never have too many friends. Most Best Friends report being intimate with up to five pillows a night.

Here is how to arrange your little slumber group: two soft pillows under your head (helps fight heartburn and a stuffy nose), one between your knees to support your loose hips and one against your tummy. There may not be much room left for your partner, but, hey, pregnancy is hard on all of us.

Notes

_____

_____

_____

_____

_____

_____

DATE _____

Go ahead and buy maternity tights and leggings. I know you think you can still squeeze into your old ones, but if you bend over or sneeze, you will find the waistband rolled up tight just above your pubic hair.

Get the ones designed for your belly.

Notes

_____

_____

_____

_____

_____

_____

DATE _____

You deserve to swim, even if you don't look like a *Sports Illustrated* swimsuit model anymore. That's why you should invest in a maternity swimsuit. By the end of this trimester, even a larger size of your traditional non-maternity suit will not be up to the job. Your belly needs more fabric than regular suits provide, plus your glorious breasts will thank you for the extra support a maternity suit provides.

Best Friends' Note: Use a hand mirror to check your pubic area; otherwise, you may be overdue for a wax or shave and not know it because your belly has hidden it.

NOTES

_____

_____

_____

_____

_____

DATE _____

Remember your first trimester, when you began to see veins where you'd never seen them before, like your breasts? Well, Best Friend, by this time, you might also have noticed them on your legs. Yes, I am doing my best to ease you into the topic of varicose veins. Quick, sit down before we go on. Yes, they look pretty ghastly, and they can hurt, but I promise things will vastly improve after the baby is born. In the meantime, invest in several pairs of maternity support tights and sit with your feet up at every possible opportunity.

NOTES

_____

_____

_____

_____

_____

_____

DATE _____

The only exercises that you must commit to are pelvic floor ones. They are intended to strengthen the muscles in your pelvic floor, which is somewhere around your vagina, cervix and bladder. This is the front line of defence against incontinence and a loose vagina after delivery.

You can identify these muscles by stopping the flow of urine when you're on the toilet. The mental image should be of a lift moving up from your labia to behind your navel. You'll know you're doing these exercises right if they make you feel a little anxious by the time the muscles get to the top floor.

NOTES

DATE _____

You know the balloon animals that clowns make at birthday parties? Take a look at your hands and feet. Notice any resemblance? That is what is known as water retention. Many pregnant women end up having to remove their rings by the third trimester because they are too tight. Consider this just another good reason to sit with your feet up and your hands idle.

Notes

_____

_____

_____

_____

_____

_____

DATE _____

Stretch marks might be artfully decorating your breasts, belly and bum, and you feel like killing the great artist on high. While these marks won't go away, they will improve tremendously in the year after the baby is born, especially if you keep them out of the sun. Just as heroes in the military earn stripes, so do the heroes of maternity, and they should be worn with at least as much pride.

NOTES

TOP 10 PREGNANCY FASHION VIOLATIONS

10. JUMPSUITS (THINK BOZO).

9. ANYTHING WITH LARGE BUTTONS IN CONTRASTING COLOURS, SAILOR COLLARS OR BIG LOOPY BOWS.

8. DRESSES OR BLOUSES BELTED.

7. CAP SLEEVES.

6. SHOULDER PADS.

5. FLAT SANDALS.

4. JACKETS THAT ARE NOT LONG ENOUGH TO COVER YOUR THIGHS.

3. TIGHTS IN ANY COLOUR OTHER THAN BLACK.

2. STIRRUPS THAT SHOW ABOVE THE SHOE.

1. T-SHIRTS WITH WITTY SAYINGS LIKE 'BABY ON BOARD' OR 'I'M NOT FAT, I'M PREGNANT!'

DATE _____

The Best Friends support legislation requiring all visibly pregnant women to wear opaque stockings, preferably black, when their legs are visible. Trust us in this, unless you are certain that you have no protruding veins, a flawless, even colour and no extra padding at the knees and thighs.

Notes

DATE _____

Let's talk about trousers with stirrups. They are ubiquitous in maternity fashion, and with good reason, because they give your legs a longer, less bumpy appearance. But there is a hard and fast rule. Never, ever, wear shoes that show the stirrup. Wear boots, or even big gym socks, but don't have that little pudgy part of your pregnant foot on display. If you can't wear boots, at least promise us that you will wear opaque tights that match the trousers.

Notes

_____

_____

_____

_____

_____

_____

DATE _____

Right about now, you may be thinking about getting a new hairdo. You know, something shorter, bouncier, easier to care for when the baby comes. STOP RIGHT THERE, BEST FRIEND! What you're looking for can't be found in any beauty parlour. No hairdresser on this planet can give you a 'do' that makes you look thin, energetic and well-rested at this point, so wait until the baby comes and your judgement is more reliable.

NOTES

_____

_____

_____

_____

_____

_____

DATE _____

Pregnancy and the need to remodel or redecorate go hand in hand. Something in the progesterone makes women want to rip up their carpets, install a walk-in shower or repaint the entire house. Whatever the project, it is guaranteed to take nearly forty weeks to accomplish, just so that it will be a dead heat which is finished first – the baby or the new living room.

NOTES

DATE _____

Itchy skin is the pregnant woman's crucible.

Gloves

With all that stretching your skin's enduring, it's a wonder it doesn't complain even more emphatically. Lotions will help, and your doctor may suggest one with an antihistamine in it. If you are clawing yourself, here is a Best Friends' tip: put on cotton gloves before you settle in for a nice scratch . . . you will be less apt to draw blood.

Notes

_____

_____

_____

_____

_____

_____

DATE _____

Here is today's addition to your pregnancy vocabulary: *acid reflux*, also known as 'heartburn'.

This nasty condition occurs when the natural closure that keeps your stomach acids down in your stomach instead of up near your throat surrenders to the pressure of your rising uterus.

If your doctor is the least bit compassionate, you will be encouraged to take antacids for relief. These chalky little morsels really do help, and you should keep them everywhere, from your handbag to your desk drawer to your glove compartment, and especially your bedside table.

NoteS

_____

_____

_____

_____

_____

DATE _ _ _ _ _ _ _ _ _ _ _ _ _

When in doubt, sit down, put your feet up and turn so that you are lying on your hip rather than your buttocks. This posture, casual though it may look, is serious medicine.

First, it gives your swaybacked spine a break.

Second, it helps in the battle against water-retaining ankles and takes a load off your back. Third, if no one has noticed you sitting there yet, you could sneak in a little nap.

NOTES

_ _

_ _

_ _

_ _

_ _

_ _

DATE _____

The Best Friends' advice for today is: 'Let your mothers into your pregnancy.' If you are fortunate enough to have a mother and/or mother-in-law on this earth, no matter how judgemental and annoying, try getting to know her on this new level.

As you become a mother, we guarantee you will gain a new tolerance and insight into why your own mother is such a nut, because you will turn into one, too. Not only will your mothers love your angel with fierce devotion . . . they may even baby-sit if begged.

Notes

_____

_____

_____

_____

_____

_____

DATE _____

If you have taken the Best Friends' advice and asked for your mother's help after the baby is born, have her come a week or two *after* the baby is born, when your adrenaline is wearing off and the baby is waking up. You and your little family deserve a few days to discover each other and set up your life without parental intrusion. Besides, babies don't even *begin* to act colicky until they are three weeks old.

NOTES

DATE _____

Thinking back on it now, do you think you know the precise moment when you conceived? Lots of otherwise rational women insist they felt something shift in the universe the instant the sperm crashed into the egg. Personally, I was so out of tune with the life cycle that I thought I was experiencing early menopause when I became pregnant with my daughter, but I don't doubt for a moment the veracity of my more cosmically conscious Best Friends.

Notes

_____

_____

_____

_____

_____

_____

DATE _____

Now is a good time to figure out your living accommodation for when you turn into a family. Given your financial situation, can you afford to move? Can you afford not to? Do you need to do some work around the house? Extra space for live-in help? Don't put these things off and don't even think about leaving this until after the baby comes, imagining you'll have so much free time – because you won't.

NOTES

_____

_____

_____

_____

_____

_____

DATE _____

Just because your partner refuses to read the pregnancy books you leave
on his side of the bed, and shows little enthusiasm for accompanying you
every month to the clinic, doesn't mean he will be an indifferent father.
Many people, men in particular, don't romanticize the biology of
pregnancy. Don't worry, he'll come around when the baby does.

Notes

_____

_____

_____

_____

_____

_____

DATE _____

Trust your Best Friends when we tell you that, even if he denies it on a
stack of Bibles, your partner secretly thinks pregnancy has made you
irrational, emotional and unpredictable . . . three things he least likes in a
person, especially you. Don't take it personally . . . he's just terrified.

NOTES

_____

_____

_____

_____

_____

_____

DATE _____

Spending way too much time reading about pregnancy so you can imagine every possible horrendous disease that could afflict your baby? Once you've worked your way through *eczema* and *heat rash*, you still have *roseola* and *scarlet fever* waiting patiently for you. As my grandmother always said, 'You don't have to buy trouble, they're giving it away for free.'

Relax and count your blessings.

P.S. Let us save you the trouble of looking up the diseases we just mentioned, you poor, frantic thing.

A DOCTOR CAN CURE ALL OF THEM!

Notes

_____

_____

_____

_____

_____

DATE _____

It's . . . exercise time! You might be so distracted and forgetful at this
point in your life that you have totally neglected your pelvic floor, but
that's what Best Friends are for. We are here to remind you that if you
want to have great orgasms, satisfy your partner sexually and refrain from
tinkling every time you sneeze, the key to that kingdom is pelvic floor
exercises. Try holding to a count of fifteen.

NOTES

_____

_____

_____

_____

_____

_____

Surrender

DATE _____

Pregnancy is a total body experience. You must be shocked on a daily basis about how much control that little tyrant in your tummy has over the rest of you. Your emotions, your complexion, your sex drive and your hair growth are all affected by your baby. This is when you must learn to surrender and realize that this child has you in its spell until the day you die.

NOTES

_____

_____

_____

_____

_____

_____

DATE _____

Now that you are starting to show, people (even total strangers . . . even
men!) will feel compelled to pat your belly. If you don't
mind, good, because you have several more months
of it coming. If you do mind, immediately cross your
arms over your tummy and explain that pregnancy
has made you incredibly ticklish and you'll wet
your pants if touched.

NOTES

_____

_____

_____

_____

_____

_____

DATE _____

One of the more jolting pregnancy experiences is leg cramps or charley horses in your calves. One minute you are in bed, and *zap* . . . the back of your lower leg feels as though it's been grabbed by a giant lobster with hot claws.

Slowly stand up and put your hands against the wall to support yourself, then step backward as far as you can stretch while keeping your heels on the floor, at an angle to the wall. Tread from one foot to the other till the mutinous muscles have relaxed, then climb back into bed, being careful not to point your toes. Some people say more calcium in your diet will help . . . but, who knows?

Notes

_____

_____

_____

_____

_____

DATE _____

During this fragile time in your life, try to avoid all news stories or made-for-TV movies that portray bad things happening to children. Pregnant women have been known to take to their beds after hearing Sally Struther's pleas. We all know the world is not a perfect place, but mums-to-be really need to focus inward on a world where they have some influence.

Notes

_____

_____

_____

_____

_____

_____

DATE _____

Snap out of it!

See, it really is a safe bet for me to assume you were in one of your trancelike states. You know what I'm talking about . . . that place where everything and everyone revolves around your pregnancy. It's like being the star of your own movie, as well as everyone else's.

NOtes

_____

_____

_____

_____

_____

_____

DATE _ _ _ _ _ _ _ _ _ _ _ _ _

Don't buy anything for your baby yet. First of all, it's considered bad luck. Second, you don't need anything now. Third, even if you do need something soon, you have no idea which brand is best and which shops have the lowest prices.

Relax. You can start accumulating stuff next month. Remember, the earlier you start spending money, the more in debt you will get because no one ever wakes up in her seventh month and announces, 'That's it! No more shopping for the baby! I have every single thing I need!'

NOTES

_____

_____

_____

_____

_____

DATE _____

Attention all you Best Friends who can't watch Mr Motivator without feeling like you should be exercising! Growing an entire human being in your belly is plenty of exertion for one woman. Besides, you're *supposed* to get fatter!

So give yourself a break and have some milk and biscuits.

Notes

_____

_____

_____

_____

_____

_____

DATE _____

If your yearning for sweets is a little out of hand, try a jelly baby.

Four of them (enough to get through a sugar crisis) are only about fifteen calories and no fat.

Better still, they mask the bad taste in your mouth when your lazy oesophagus has been leaking your lunch for the last hour. Sure, fruit is even better, but you don't need me to tell you that.

Notes

_____

_____

_____

_____

_____

_____

DATE _ _ _ _ _ _ _ _ _ _ _ _ _

You're right . . . it was your partner who did this to you, and he owes you

endless hours of attention and pampering!

Notes

_ _

_ _

_ _

_ _

_ _

_ _

DATE _____

Repeat this over and over until you believe it:

'My due date means nothing. My due date means nothing.'

Remember, the magical date the midwife divines on that adorable little cardboard wheel is just an estimation, not a booking like a haircut or a plane flight. You cannot plan your days around it like you would around elective surgery. Get used to the baby having this kind of influence over you . . . it will continue for the rest of your life.

Notes

_____

_____

_____

_____

_____

_____

DATE _____

The universe is just not fair. If you accept that,
you will be better able to accept that it is, indeed,
possible for PMS to last forty weeks. Don't ask,
'Why me?'

You don't want to go there . . . just tear open
another bag of taco-flavoured crisps and forget about it.

NoteS

_____

_____

_____

_____

_____

_____

DATE _____

Whenever you are driving and you come to a red light, do a pelvic floor exercise and try to hold it until the light turns green. This may seem impossible at first, especially at busy junctions, but it's a goal. Remember, we're fighting giggle-peeing here, not to mention trying to preserve your future sex life.

NOTES

_____

_____

_____

_____

_____

_____

DATE _____

Have you had a moment of questionable judgement when you actually
considered having a home birth? Put that thought right out of your head,
especially if this is your first child. Delivery is grisly business. Why would
you want to ruin your mattress and beautiful sheets? Don't worry, you'll
be home soon enough.

Notes

_____

_____

_____

_____

_____

_____

DATE _____

Appetites are ferocious in pregnant women.
You're never 'just a little hungry', and you never
'sort of' have to go to the bathroom. This is the 'I want it and I want it
now' phase of pregnancy.

NOTES

DATE _____

Are you in a group practice and do you hate one of the doctors? And are you sure you're going to get him when it's time to deliver? Short of a scheduled C-section, which is a bit extreme, it's a lot like Russian roulette. Look at the bright side. If you hate the doctor, you'll have very few compunctions about screaming at him in the delivery room, when doctors make their guest appearances. Worry more about the midwives; they'll be with you every step of the way and by the end are often honorary Best Friends.

Notes

_____
_____
_____
_____
_____
_____

SECOND TRIMESTER 94 DAYS TO GO

DATE _____

Take a good look at your partner's wardrobe, if you haven't already. He may have some white dress shirts, big sweaters, vests or baggy jeans that you can use during your maternity fashion crisis. Help yourself, but don't freak out if they're too tight.

NOTES

DATE _____

Has it dawned on you yet that no matter how hard it is to have this baby inside you, the job will only get harder when it comes out?

NOTES

_____

_____

_____

_____

_____

_____

DATE _____

Thanks to modern science and age-old curiosity, there is a good chance that you already know the gender of your baby. If it's a boy, your immediate obsession should now be CIRCUMCISION (or not).* You can't start sharing your concerns and fears with your partner a minute too soon. I guarantee, this is one aspect of pregnancy that is certain to get his attention and keep it for a nice long time.

* Circumcision is often carried out in the US for aesthetic or traditional reasons; in the UK it is rare except for cultural or religious reasons.

Notes

_____

_____

_____

_____

_____

_____

DATE _____

Heartburn does not mean that your baby will be born with lots of hair. You can have heartburn so badly that you spit fire, and your baby can still come out as bald as Telly Savalas. This condition gets progressively worse as the baby pushes open your oesophagus. Remember, keep those antacids handy. They work better than a fire extinguisher.

Notes

DATE _____

Feeling a little funky? Buy yourself two or three of those tabloid magazines and cut out unattractive photos of pregnant celebrities. Tape them to your bathroom mirror for easy reference.

NOTES

_____

_____

_____

_____

_____

_____

DATE _____

Do you have the sneaking suspicion that you are getting a crush on your doctor? This is quite common, particularly if he is a man. Think about it, he is one of the few people left on this earth who still seems interested in how you feel. He is also the only thing that stands between you and what you secretly believe is certain death because you know that labour and delivery survival does not lie in focus objects, funny breathing or your partner rolling tennis balls on your lower back.

Notes

_____

_____

_____

_____

_____

_____

DATE _____

It may be impossible for you to fully grasp at this juncture in your life, but right now it is ridiculous for you to make any informed decisions regarding vaginal births vs. caesarean sections*, pain medication vs. relaxation techniques or rooming-in vs. leaving the baby in the hospital nursery while you sleep. You haven't a clue yet about how you will feel or what surprises labour and delivery have in store for you. Whatever you do, don't expect your experience to be anything like your 'prepared childbirth'** teacher describes (she doesn't want to alarm you) or like you've seen on TV, because those shows are invariably written by childless bachelors.

* Elective caesareans are less common in the UK than in the US.
** More usually called antenatal or parentcraft classes in the UK.

NOTES

_____

_____

_____

_____

_____

coffee break

DATE _____

You should start thinking now about who you want to go to the hospital with you. Of course, your partner should be at the top of the list, but you might want to invite your mother, sister or Best Friend. You see, labour often lasts a very long time, and after a few hours men tend to annoy their contracting partners. Almost every woman in deep labour pauses mid-contraction at some point to yell accusingly, 'You did this to me!' or 'Stop breathing around me; I can't stand the turbulence.'

This is a good time for Dad to get a cup of coffee and have the women-folk step in for a while.

NOTES

_____

_____

_____

_____

_____

_____

86

Boy? girl?

DATE _____

'You're carrying so high, it must be a boy.'

'You're positively glowing, it must be a girl.'

You may have noticed by now that guessing the gender of your baby is a favourite hobby for the public at large. Just wait until someone talks you into lying on your back while they dangle your wedding ring from a piece of thread over your belly. If it moves in a clockwise manner, you're having one sex, and if it moves anti-clockwise, you're having the other. I guess if it moves in a figure eight, you're having an ice-skater.

NOTES

DATE _____

Consider registering at a baby department, like brides do at department stores. When people ask what you want 'for the baby', you will be protected from receiving fifteen darling little cardigans with matching blankets. After the baby is born, have a few of your close friends spread the word that you're registered, because there is nothing worse than having someone else pick out your changing bag.

Notes

_____

_____

_____

_____

_____

_____

THIRD TRIMESTER 84 DAYS TO GO

DATE _____

It's time for a detached appraisal of your wardrobe.
Those cute little dresses that you have been living
in may now be so short at the front from your
protruding tummy and so long at the back from your pregnant swayback
that you look like you're tipping over. Same thing applies to tunics,
sweaters and T-shirts. Either restrict your wardrobe to long dresses or
commit to maternity clothes from here on in. Trust me.

NOTES

_____
_____
_____
_____
_____
_____

DATE _ _ _ _ _ _ _ _ _ _ _ _ _

You have probably received enough unsolicited advice to drive you mad. Don't people understand – pregnancy alone can inspire madness?

Here are a few things to keep in mind:

1. Never believe anything a man tells you (unless he is a doctor). He doesn't have a uterus. He has never directly experienced PMS, let alone labour.

2. Keep in mind that most women were high on pain medication when they delivered their babies, so they might not remember the event with great accuracy.

3. Situations that are routine to doctors seem like matters of life and death to first-time parents.

NOTES

_____

_____

_____

_____

DATE _____

Let's be grown-ups here for a moment, OK? Toward the end of your pregnancy, you may learn that every single thing does not necessarily go according to the maternity plan you have lovingly and optimistically concocted. For example, you might be put on bed rest for a while, or the baby might be stubbornly staying in the breech position, or maybe your blood pressure is getting a little higher than you and your doctor would like.

This is not the time to be a big baby. Just do what the doctor tells you and stop pouting. This happens to a lot of us. Remember, you're still going to end up with a perfect baby.

NOTES

DATE _____

Try not to sit in one position too long. Long car rides, sitting at a desk or parking yourself in front of a TV can nearly stop the blood in your legs from circulating back to your heart if you don't move around every so often. Imagine holding a bowling ball in your lap for a couple of hours. Same concept.

Get up and stretch at least once an hour. You can always use this opportunity to go to the toilet.

Notes

_____

_____

_____

_____

_____

_____

DATE _____

Let's talk about haemorrhoids. These are, for you blessedly uninitiated, little lumps in and around the anus created by blood vessels pooling up and herniating. They are particularly popular among pregnant women and new mums.

If not for pregnancy, you might have lived your entire life blissfully ignorant of these little grape clusters. Between your growing baby cutting off your circulation, not to mention your pushing too hard when constipated, and labour, it's hard to avoid this painful humiliation.

P.S. They go away eventually, only to flare up occasionally or with your next pregnancy.

Notes

DATE --------------

It may be a little over the top to play classical music near your pregnant belly or for your partner to read the classics to it, but babies really do hear you from inside the womb. Just watch after the baby is born; it will quieten to hear Mummy's or Daddy's voice. Of course, it will get to know your voices throughout your entire pregnancy as it eavesdrops on all nearby conversations, whether you are speaking directly to the little sweetie or not. Consider this an inkling of what you have to look forward to as a parent.

NOTES

DATE _____

Buy or rent a pager for your partner. Both of you will be understandably nervous about labour starting and your being unable to reach him, especially in this era of voice mail and other non-human impediments to telephone communication.

Go ahead and test him with a false alarm, but only ONCE. Sure it will scare the hell out of him, but hey, we're all scared, so beep away (ONCE!).

Notes

_____

_____

_____

_____

_____

_____

DATE _____

The male population is easily divided into two camps: those who are aroused by big pregnant women, and those who are scared to death by them. You and your partner are probably right now in the midst of discovering into which category he falls. Some guys love the luscious ripeness of a pregnant woman, and others find it problematic having sex with someone who now outweighs them. Don't worry about it. Either you will become the sunshine of his life or you and your vibrator are about to start a meaningful relationship.

NOTES

_____

_____

_____

_____

_____

_____

Jade

DATE _____

Try to decide on the baby's name before delivery. Labour is not a good time to make any important decisions. I'll never understand people who say they want to see the baby first; if that was the case, the top names would be ET and Kojak.

Jessica

Jeremy

Jamie

Notes

DATE _____

Unless you live in Polynesia, avoid the temptation to wear sandals to relieve the water retention in your sad little feet, especially if it's winter. There must be a deck shoe or trainer out there somewhere that you fit into without feeling like one of Cinderella's wicked stepsisters. Fat, swollen feet are rarely attractive and should be hidden at all costs.

NoteS

_____

_____

_____

_____

_____

_____

DATE _____

Don't forget to wash your feet and cut your toenails regularly. Out of sight, out of mind applies in the personal hygiene department, and you probably haven't seen your feet for weeks.

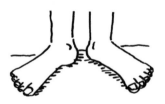

NOTES

_____

_____

_____

_____

_____

_____

DATE _____

Does it come as any surprise that, like several of your other organs, your bowels have turned against you in your time of need? Yes, we're talking about constipation. The first step toward a cure is to up your water and fibre intake. Then check with your doctor to ask whether an iron supplement in your antenatal vitamins* could be contributing to the logjam. While you have him or her on the line, you might also request a suggestion for a stool softener. In the meantime, pay attention to the muscles you use to have a 'movement' because they are the same ones you'll use to deliver the baby. Bet nobody ever told you that before!

* Antenatal vitamin supplements are not routinely recommended in the UK.

notes

_____

_____

_____

_____

DATE --------------

There is really no use making up dream labour scenarios, whether they include flawless Lamaze breathing or drugs on demand, because this experience is nothing if not surprising. If you get too hooked on a preconceived (no pun intended) notion of a 'perfect' way for your child to enter this world, you're setting a standard that is rigid, judgemental and uninformed. Remember, no matter whether you deliver your child alone in a rice paddy or receive it via Federal Express, it is a 'perfect' delivery.

NOTES

DATE _____

Be extra careful getting up from chairs or out of bed. Your hip ligaments may be loosening up in preparation for passing a head the size of a melon through them. That loose-hipped condition can give you the sensation of having rubber legs, and it's easy to fall. Imagine the sensation of having ridden a horse for the last couple of days and you'll have some idea of the challenge here.

Notes

_____

_____

_____

_____

_____

_____

powder

DATE _____

Put talcum powder everywhere on your body that skin touches skin. This could take some time. Start with your substantial upper arms; they rub against your breasts and sides with every step you take. Then move on to where your breasts rest on your belly; that's usually as damp as the tropics. And how about those thighs? There is so much friction between them you could light a campfire without a match.

Notes

_____

_____

_____

_____

_____

_____

DATE _____

Aren't parties a bore now? No sexy little black dresses, no wine or salty margaritas. Even the hors d'oeuvres give you heartburn. You will now learn something that every practising member of a twelve-step programme already knows: drunk people are incredibly tiresome if you're not one of them.

The Best Friends' suggestion? Stay at home and catch up on some sleep.

Notes

_____

_____

_____

_____

_____

_____

DATE --------------

Somewhere between 15 and 30 per cent of all American deliveries are by caesarean section,* depending on your doctor and the hospital in which you deliver. This is a fact, not a judgement, since I think any relatively painless method of giving birth is just swell, but it is an indication that you should be flexible in your expectations about what lies ahead of you. There is a fairly good chance that your baby will not emerge after one hour of hee-hee breathing and a couple of good pushes. You will be the hero no matter what happens and your baby will be spectacular and, really, isn't that all that matters?

* Around 10 per cent in the UK.

NOTES

DATE _____

If you wear contact lenses, you may find that the prescription seems off.
There is so much water being retained in your body and your blood
vessels are so dilated that your eyeballs can actually change shape
enough to fuzz up your vision. Don't throw your contacts away, however,
because they will fit again after the baby is born. Unlike your feet and
other unmentionable body parts, your eyes will go back to normal.

Notes

_____

_____

_____

_____

_____

_____

DATE _____

Beware of the Pregnancy Police, Best Friend. These are the folks who feel obligated to look into your shopping trolley and comment if you have diet coke or something with preservatives in it. They also park themselves in airports near the security checks to make sure you don't walk through the metal detectors. Their favourite haunts, however, are restaurants where they lie in wait for a pregnant woman to sip some wine. Then they pounce on her, spewing factoids about foetal alcohol syndrome. These people are not well-intentioned, they are just busybodies and deserve to be ignored.

NOTES

_____

_____

_____

_____

_____

DATE _ _ _ _ _ _ _ _ _ _ _ _ _

Some of you already know by this time that you are going to have a caesarean section. Perhaps the baby is really big, or you have a little herpes outbreak or some other reason why a vaginal birth isn't going to work out.

Caesareans, particularly those that are elective, can be at least as rewarding and thrilling as vaginal births. There is something wonderful about knowing when your baby is coming. You can drive relatively calmly to the hospital, you will be perfectly groomed *and* you get to keep the vagina of a teenager.

Notes

_____

_____

_____

_____

_____

_____

THIRD TRIMESTER 64 DAYS TO GO

DATE _____

Prepare a list of names and phone numbers of the people you want your partner to call after the baby is born, and pack it in your suitcase. He will be delirious and certainly won't have a phone book, and you will probably be eating or sleeping by this time.

The rule of thumb regarding phone calls is this: call all immediate relatives and close friends who've had kids as soon as possible, day or night.

Call all childless friends before 10 P.M. or after 9 A.M.; they may not be able to comprehend the sheer miraculousness of the event if they are awakened from a deep sleep.

Notes

_____

_____

_____

_____

_____

_____

DATE _____

Beg a mum Best Friend to accompany you and your partner to a baby department when you're ready to buy furniture and other equally mystifying infant necessities.

YOU DON'T NEED EVERYTHING ON THE SHOWROOM FLOOR, and you'll want a more disinterested party than the salesperson to guide you. Short of delivery itself, this can be one of the scariest aspects of pregnancy (and that's *before* you get the bill!).

Notes

_____

_____

_____

_____

_____

_____

TOP 10 THINGS TO TAKE TO THE HOSPITAL

10. YOUR PARTNER. HE'S NOT ESSENTIAL, BUT IT'S NICE TO HAVE SOMEONE TO BLAME FOR YOUR MISERY. A BEST FRIEND MIGHT BE FUN TO GIVE YOUR PARTNER A CAFETERIA BREAK EVERY NOW AND THEN.

9. LIP BALM. EVEN THOUGH IT'S YOUR OTHER LIPS THAT ARE SEEING ALL THE ACTION DURING DELIVERY, THE LIPS ON YOUR MOUTH TEND TO GET VERY DRY, ESPECIALLY IF YOU TRY ANY EXOTIC BREATHING TECHNIQUES.

8. YOUR OWN PILLOWS IN OLD PILLOWCASES. NOT ONLY ARE THEY INFINITELY MORE COMFORTABLE THAN HOSPITAL-ISSUE, THEY SMELL LIKE HOME AND THAT CAN BE A COMFORT AMIDST ALL THE SURGICAL AROMAS IN A LABOUR AND DELIVERY ROOM.

7. CAMERAS, BOTH VIDEO AND STILL, WITH EXTRA FILM FOR BOTH. MAKE SURE THAT YOU HAVE CHARGED THE VIDEO CAM'S BATTERIES AND HAVE BROUGHT AN EXTRA BECAUSE YOU MAY USE UP ALL YOUR POWER BEFORE THE GUEST OF HONOUR ARRIVES.

6. EXTRA SOCKS. FOOTSIES GET COLD DURING LABOUR. THE MIDWIFE WILL LET YOU KEEP THEM ON THROUGH DELIVERY, TOO, BUT THEY MAY GET A LITTLE BLOODY AT THAT POINT, SO HAVE SEVERAL PAIRS TO REPLACE THEM AS NEEDED.

5. FOOD AND WATER. SOME FRUIT BARS OR TRAIL MIX, MAYBE SOME POPCORN, CAN COME IN VERY HANDY AFTER DELIVERY WHEN YOU'RE STARVING, BUT THE HOSPITAL'S NOT SERVING. BOTTLED WATER IS ALWAYS TASTIER THAN THE STUFF THEY PUT IN THE LITTLE PLASTIC PITCHER ON YOUR BEDSIDE TABLE.

4. YOUR GLASSES, IF YOU USUALLY WEAR CONTACTS. A COUPLE OF GOOD PUSHES CAN SEND CONTACTS FLYING ACROSS THE ROOM, BUT YOU MAY WANT TO GET A GOOD LOOK AT THE BABY WHEN IT COMES.

3. MATERNITY CLOTHES TO WEAR HOME FROM THE HOSPITAL. SORRY, BUT YOU WILL STILL BE FAT. BESIDES, YOU WILL NEED THE GIGANTIC PANTS TO HOLD THE MANY SANITARY PADS YOU WILL BE WEARING FOR THE NEXT FEW DAYS. THIS INCLUDES A NURSING BRA IF YOU INTEND TO GIVE THAT A TRY.

2. YOUR OWN TOILETRIES, INCLUDING SHAMPOO, SOAP, LOTION AND TOOTHPASTE. OF CRITICAL IMPORTANCE ARE MAKEUP AND YOUR OWN HAIR-DRYER; REMEMBER, IT'S A PHOTO FREE-FOR-ALL ONCE THE BABY ARRIVES.

1. A LIST OF NAMES AND PHONE NUMBERS IN ORDER OF IMPORTANCE AND A PHONECARD SO YOUR PARTNER CAN USE THE PAY PHONES WITHOUT CARRYING MORE CHANGE THAN A SLOT MACHINE ATTENDANT.

DATE _____

You may have noticed a yellowish liquid leaking from your breasts when you squeeze them (don't we all spend our free time squeezing our own breasts?). If you have, congratulations, you are making colostrum, the premilk food breastfed babies eat for the first couple of days of life. If your squeezing isn't yielding anything, or if you just prefer not to squeeze, don't fret; the colostrum is in there anyway.

NOTES

DATE _____

Should you breastfeed? Our best answer is this: don't do it unless you
really want to. This is not something you must try just because your
Lamaze teacher told you to. Here is another area in which you have the
Best Friends' full understanding and support if you ignore all societal
pressure and do what is specifically right for you and your unique
circumstances. Breastfeeding is great. For some people, it is better than
orgasm and lasts longer. But you can live a full and wonderful life never
having hung one single human from your breasts. If you don't believe me,
just ask your mother.

NOTES

_____

_____

_____

_____

_____

_____

DATE _____

The nappy debate rages on: cloth or disposable? Your choice here will not affect your overall grade in Motherhood, so relax. Here's our general guideline: if you live in an arid area that is prone to droughts, use disposables because you won't waste water washing them. If you live near Niagara Falls or in a rain forest, use cloth and keep the landfill dumping to a minimum. There, wasn't that easy?

Notes

_____

_____

_____

_____

_____

_____

DATE _____

Select your baby announcements today. You can pick
one for a boy and one for a girl if you don't yet know which you're having,
but make sure that the envelopes are the same for both. That way you
can take the envelopes and start addressing them *now*, not when you are
sitting on a haemorrhoid pillow or trying to learn to feed a crying baby.
When the baby comes, call the printer with pertinent information or fill it
out yourself sometime between birth and the child's first birthday. Both of
these jobs, by the way, are ambisexirous – meaning they can be done by
Dads, too.

NOTES

_____

_____

_____

_____

_____

_____

DATE _____

Today is a good day to go lingerie shopping. Before you and your partner get too excited, let me clarify that the lingerie you need consists of a couple of nursing bras with peek-a-boo cups and several pairs of cheap maternity pants. Don't howl! They will be your friends for quite some time. Contrary to your illusions, you will still be using maternity pants after the baby is several weeks (if not months) old. First, you'll still be chubby; second, you'll need a serious undergarment to hold all those sanitary pads; and third, a G-string or thong panties after a vaginal birth will sound about as appealing as a wad of bubble gum after root canal surgery.

NOTES

_____

_____

_____

_____

_____

_____

DATE _____

Do not insist that your partner cut the umbilical cord or take a long and loving look at the placenta, even though your midwife will probably offer both opportunities. If he wants to, fine. If his upper lip gets sweaty at the suggestion, allow him to decline. This is no time to ruin the moment with arguments and disappointments. Save them for the first day home from the hospital.

Notes

_____

_____

_____

_____

_____

_____

DATE -------------

Upsetting stories abound about labouring women being given enemas before delivery. I would rather carry that baby in utero for the rest of my life than have an enema.

The great news is this is one indignity you don't have to endure. In fact, several of my Best Friends were never even offered the chance to decline; nobody suggested it to them. I think there used to be a worry that if you pushed hard to get the baby out, some poopoo would come out, too. Well, that does indeed happen, but since they don't come out of the same opening, nobody really cares. And neither should you.

NOTES

THIRD TRIMESTER 55 DAYS TO GO

DATE _____

All seriously pregnant women get the desperate urge to
pee and frantically run to the bathroom, only to find that
a tiny trickle comes out when they sit down. If
you think that you have had pregnancy up to here,
just pause to think how your little pancake of a bladder must be feeling
about now.

Notes

_____

_____

_____

_____

_____

_____

DATE _____

You should be looking into available prepared childbirth classes right about now. You will get a big kick out of them at first, then learn to feel trapped and pressured by them. Your partner will dislike them at the beginning and be openly hostile by the end . . . but they're as much a part of pregnancy as stretch marks.

NOTES

_____

_____

_____

_____

_____

_____

DATE _____

Don't let the Best Friends' affection for epidurals make you think that we
don't believe in antenatal classes.

First of all, pain avoidance through controlled breathing is a wonderful
skill to have, especially for bikini waxes or any dental procedure where
the dentist says, 'This will only sting for a minute.' Second, it can be fun
to get in a room full of other butterballs . . . and third, classes can be
fulfilling for those people who just can't see enough grainy movies of
complete strangers giving birth.

NOTES

_____

_____

_____

_____

_____

_____

DATE _____

Many of us Best Friends suffered the ultimate indignity of having our belly buttons pop out during our last few weeks of pregnancy. It can make a very noticeable bump, even through a blouse or dress, and you will panic if someone comes toward you with an outstretched hand ready to pat your belly. Best Friends' tip: put a thick plaster over your belly button and then wear maternity tights whenever you leave your house. That ought to flatten things out sufficiently.

NOTES

_____

_____

_____

_____

_____

_____

DATE _____

You may feel jumpy now that labour and delivery are within spitting distance.

Take a deep breath and try to relax. Oh, we forgot, you can't take deep breaths anymore. In fact, you're so full of baby that you are claustrophobic.

We promise you will get immediate relief the instant the baby appears.

NOTES

_____

_____

_____

_____

_____

_____

DATE _____

Here is another phrase for your pregnancy vocabulary: 'vagina farts'.
These little emissions occur when the baby is large, head down, and
pressing against your cervix so hard that it feels like your labia are down
around your knees.

Walking, bending over, lifting – whatever – work like a bellows, sucking in
and puffing out little bubbles of air, unfortunately accompanied by
raspberry sounds. Just act shocked and look around as if wondering what
boor had the gall to make such a noise.

NOTES

_____

_____

_____

_____

_____

_____

DATE _____

It's getting harder and harder to eat now. Your stomach is smashed up flat as a pancake under your rib cage, and even though you are constantly hungry, you are full after two bites.

Think of yourself as a hummingbird (don't laugh, I could have said cow), and just take sips (or graze) throughout the entire day. You may even lose a pound or two just before delivery as your appetite continues to shrink. Don't worry, you'll eat like a lumberjack as soon as your baby arrives and you have flagged down a nurse (or maybe your partner!) to bring you some food.

Notes

_____

_____

_____

_____

_____

_____

DATE _____

Sleeping is getting harder and harder with every week, right? Some hopeless optimists (usually childless) will tell you that this is nature's way of getting you used to the scarcity of sleep you will experience as a new mother. What a crock!

That's like saying dieting prepares you for starvation.

You aren't sleeping because there is only room for one of you in this body, pardner.

Notes

_____

_____

_____

_____

_____

_____

DATE _____

Pedicures should be particularly important to you now. Think about it . . . what part of your body will be closest to your doctor or midwife's face during check-ups and delivery? WRONG!!! I'm talking about your feet. You may not notice them yourself at this point, hidden as they are by your belly, but don't get negligent about this critical area of grooming.

If you have the extra time and money, indulge in a professional pedicure. First of all, you probably can't reach your toes yourself; and, second, your bloated feet could use a massage.

Notes

_____

_____

_____

_____

_____

_____

TOP 10 CHANGES TO YOUR BODY

10. YOUR FEET ARE SWOLLEN AND LARGER, AND THE BAD NEWS IS THAT THEY MAY PERMANENTLY GROW AN EXTRA SHOE SIZE. THE GOOD NEWS IS THAT IT DOESN'T HAPPEN WITH EACH SUBSEQUENT BIRTH.

9. YOUR DIGESTIVE SYSTEM IS SLIGHTLY DYSFUNC- TIONAL. BETWEEN WIND AND HEART-BURN, YOU CAN HARDLY STAND TO BE AROUND YOURSELF.

8. YOU WILL BE CHANGING COLOURS IN ALL SORTS OF PLACES, NOT JUST TURNING GREEN. FROM YOUR NIPPLES TO YOUR LABIA, THERE'S NO TELLING WHERE THIS WILL TURN UP.

7. FLASHING BACK TO PUBERTY? IT'S JUST PREGNANCY PIMPLES. YOUR COMPLEXION, LIKE THE REST OF YOUR BODY, MAY CHANGE COLOUR AND BECOME BLOTCHY TO BOOT. IF YOU'RE ONE OF THE 'LUCKY' ONES, YOU MAY GET TINY FLAPS OF EXTRA SKIN, USUALLY UNDER YOUR ARM OR ON THE EYELID.

6. TWO WORDS: STRETCH MARKS. WE HAVE NO WORDS OF WISDOM, JUST ANOTHER THING TO BLAME YOUR MOTHER FOR – THEY'RE HEREDITARY.

5. LUXURIOUS HAIR AND NAILS – PLAY THEM UP, THEY CAN HIDE A MULTITUDE OF SINS.

4. YOUR BUM IS GETTING LARGER. DON'T WORRY, THE BABY'S NOT GROWING THE WRONG WAY, THOUGH IT MAY FEEL LIKE THAT.

3. WATER RETENTION WITH NOWHERE TO DRAIN (IT ALMOST MAKES YOU LONG FOR YOUR PERIOD). YOUR ENTIRE BODY IS PUFFIER, FROM YOUR NOSE TO YOUR TOES.

2. BIG BOUNCING BREASTS THAT WILL CONTINUE TO BLOOM ALL NINE (TEN) MONTHS.

1. OVERWHELMING BODILY FUNCTIONS, WITH THE WINNER BEING PEEING. A CLOSE RUNNER-UP IS CONSTIPATION.

DATE _____

Women approaching their due date are worried sick that they will go into labour and not recognize it. The thought of going to the hospital and being told it was a false alarm becomes the highest form of humiliation imaginable.

Let the Best Friends reassure you right away that far more humiliating things are in store for you. Even more to the point, consider all trips to the hospital that don't result in the birth of a baby very valuable dress rehearsals for the real opening night (pun intended).

Notes

_____

_____

_____

_____

_____

_____

DATE _____

This is just another reminder to keep up with your pelvic floor exercises. You may think we are making a big deal out of something that could turn out to be a great spoof like being invited to watch the submarine races or waiting for the salmon to spawn, but this is real, we promise.

I don't care what you hear to the contrary, if you don't keep toned in there, your career as a trampoline artist is history because your bladder will fail at every bounce.

Notes

_____

_____

_____

_____

_____

_____

DATE _ _ _ _ _ _ _ _ _ _ _ _

Take your own pillows to the hospital. Since it is still traditional for women to spend a lot of labour in bed, you will definitely prefer your own fluffy friends to the cardboard institutional pillows you will be issued.

A less obvious but very important quality your pillows have is that they smell like home. That familiar scent and feeling can be immeasurably reassuring at a time like this.

Notes

_____

_____

_____

_____

_____

_____

DATE _____

The arrival of a new baby is the greatest photo opportunity on the planet. You will probably want to record this event both on still film and on video. Guess what?

You will be in almost every picture!

If you want to look at these pictures in years to come without humiliation, consider applying light, waterproof makeup and washing and styling your hair before going to the hospital. Trust me, as superficial as this advice may sound today, you will thank me with flowers and gifts when your pictures come back from the developers. If your makeup has run and smeared, my number is unlisted.

Notes

_____

_____

_____

_____

THIRD TRIMESTER 42 DAYS TO GO

DATE _____

You and your partner should take a practice run to the [ ] hospital sometime soon. Pick your route and stick to it. One major cause of delivery panic is when there are too many options and a rational decision must be made. It is wise to eliminate all multiple-choice questions in areas related to this baby as soon as possible.

Notes

_____
_____
_____
_____
_____
_____

DATE _____

You must have a good car seat.

It is against the law in most states for a hospital to release a baby until you have shown them that you have a car seat ready for it.* This is a good rule, not only because it keeps the baby safe for the ride home, but it's a good way of identifying nincompoop parents who haven't fully adjusted to their new responsibilities. Since you will probably need two sizes of car seats during the next four years of your baby's life, make sure one is the infant model that snaps into a frame in the car and snaps out to become a baby carrier.

That way you don't wake the baby moving it from the car to the house – a crucial feature.

* This is not the case in the UK, but by law your baby must be restrained in a car seat appropriate to his or her age and weight.

Notes

_____

_____

_____

DATE _____

Do not go shopping for a beautiful nightgown and robe to wear in the hospital after the baby is born. You will only be in the hospital for what will seem like minutes, and you will still be leaking all sorts of yucky stuff that stains.

Save your nightie for your own home, and bleed all over the hospital's gowns and sheets.

That's what they're there for.

NOTES

_____

_____

_____

_____

_____

_____

DATE _____

Time to start baby-proofing your home. Sure, you can wait a few months before you begin double-locking your cabinets and putting gates at the top of the stairs, since few newborns walk immediately. But do evaluate your home from the point of view of a pure little baby. Get rid of poisonous plants, prevent accumulation of pet hair, have the heating ducts cleaned out and the system checked by a professional to make sure the gas doesn't leak or the electrical wires aren't frazzled. If you have pets, make sure they can't knock over the crib or baby carrier (in other words, get them used to the outdoors now).

NOTES

_____

_____

_____

_____

_____

_____

DATE _____

Today's new phrase for the pregnancy vocabulary is *mucous plug*. This squishy cork sits in the opening of your cervix, protecting the baby from germs. The mucous plug is made out of what the name suggests, with a pinkish blood colour.

When the cervix stretches and flattens in preparation for birth, the cork can slide out. Don't worry, it is completely painless. In fact, you probably won't even notice unless you happen to glance down before you flush. Call your doctor or midwife, but there's no need to go rushing to the hospital because you may still have several days more to go. Keep in mind, many of us don't lose our plugs until the babies push them out with their heads.

NOTES

_____

_____

_____

_____

_____

DATE --------------

It's time to pack your bag now, even if you swear it's too soon.
Remember, if you go into labour before you've packed, your partner will
be left with that job. Can't you just see him walking into the hospital with
a shopping bag under his arm filled with something sleeveless, too-tight
jeans, and no underwear or deodorant?

Notes

DATE _____

It is easier for a turtle to turn from its back to its belly than for a very
pregnant woman to roll over in her sleep. Buy or borrow one of those
total body pillows to use until D day. Hold on to it like it's a crocodile and
you're Paul Hogan. Give a big rock-and-roll motion to get the momentum
necessary to turn the two of you over. Your partner may feel a little
alienated. Then again, he may be relieved that your needs are being met
by something other than him.

NOTES

_____

_____

_____

_____

_____

_____

DATE _ _ _ _ _ _ _ _ _ _ _ _ _

We know you know this, but it bears repeating right about now. Your due date is nothing more than an estimation. Very few butterballs actually pop on that very date, and you probably won't either. Try not to drive yourself crazy expecting that day to bring relief from this never-ending condition of pregnancy, because odds are that you will be early and caught off-guard, or late and pissed off.

NoteS

_____

_____

_____

_____

_____

_____

DATE _____

If you intend to breastfeed your baby, it's about time for you to look into renting an electric breast pump.* All breastfeeding mothers with lives know that a stock of pumped milk in the freezer is better than money in the bank. It gives them freedom to take a nap or go to the shops without fearing that their little darling will starve or be forced to move on to formula.

Look in the Yellow Pages or ask at the clinic for a number.

* These are available to hire in the UK, too, but less common than in the US.

NOTES

_____

_____

_____

_____

_____

_____

DATE _____

This is a very stressful time for most men. They have watched enough old movies to know that babies arrive with great unpredictability, with the men invariably panicking and speeding off into the night, leaving the labouring mother standing in the drive beside her little suitcase.

He's like a child who knows that something is hiding somewhere in the house and he has no idea what cupboard it will pop out of. Help the poor guy out and remind him that babies, especially first babies, usually give plenty of warning before exploding into our world.

Notes

_____

_____

_____

_____

_____

_____

THIRD TRIMESTER 32 DAYS TO GO

DATE _ _ _ _ _ _ _ _ _ _ _ _ _

Uh-oh! The baby doesn't seem to be moving as often or as vigorously. You imagine the very worst, but your fear has you too paralysed to even call the doctor.

The baby is fine! As it gets bigger, there is less room for it to get a good kick in, and as it settles head-down in preparation for birth, it really feels jammed.

Do us all a favour and call your doctor immediately – not because something is wrong, but because they will have you come in and check you out. It will be a tremendous relief for everyone, particularly those who live with you.

NOTES

_____

_____

_____

_____

_____

DATE _____

Sometime near your due date, your doctor may give you something called a 'non-stress test'.*

This refers to the baby's not being stressed – *you* are stressed by nearly everything these days. This test consists of your lying down with a foetal monitor around your belly.

This will record your baby's heart rate when it moves and show whether it is strong and ready to blast into this world.

* More common in the UK if your baby is overdue or there are other causes for concern.

Notes

_____

_____

_____

_____

_____

DATE _____

About now, the internal exams begin again. The doctor or midwife will be looking inside you for signs of dilation and effacement. You will be looking for the doctor or midwife, who will doubtless be carrying on a conversation with you, and you won't be able to see him or her because your belly completely blocks your line of vision.

Notes

_____

_____

_____

_____

_____

_____

DATE _ _ _ _ _ _ _ _ _ _ _ _ _

Now is a good time for a pre-baby party if you intend to have one. You have time to kill, you deserve a major distraction and you can spend the next few days and weeks washing the clothes in Persil or decorating the nursery with the adorable stuff you have received.

NOteS

_____

_____

_____

_____

_____

_____

TOP **10** SIGNS THAT YOU MAY BE GOING INTO LABOUR

10. DIARRHOEA OR FLU-LIKE SYMPTOMS. YOUR BODY MAY
DO SOME SERIOUS SPRING CLEANING OF ITS OWN IN
ANTICIPATION OF THE BABY'S ARRIVAL.

9. FRENZIED, OBSESSIVE CLEANING AND ORGANIZING. IF
YOU GET UP AT 2 A.M. WITH AN IRRESISTIBLE NEED TO
SEW NAME LABELS IN THE BABY'S VESTS, YOU MAY BE
ABOUT TO POP.

8. YOU'VE STOPPED EATING. FEW THINGS LOOK
APPETIZING, AND NOTHING IS REALLY DIGESTING AT
THIS POINT. ICE CUBES HAVE BECOME YOUR MEAL OF
CHOICE.

7. YOU JUST FOUND A SLIMY, BLOODY HUNK OF MUCUS IN
YOUR PANTS OR IN THE TOILET. (YOUR MUCUS PLUG
CAN COME OUT WHEN YOU START DILATING AND
EFFACING.)

6. YOU ARE WETTING YOUR PANTS, AND YOU CAN'T STOP
(A SIGN THAT THE SAC OF AMNIOTIC FLUID HAS BURST,
OR YOUR 'WATERS HAVE BROKEN').

5. YOUR HAIR IS DIRTY, YOU HAVEN'T
DONE ANY WASHING IN TEN DAYS AND
THE CAR NEEDS PETROL. GUARANTEED
TO GO INTO LABOUR TONIGHT.

4. YOUR LOWER BACK HURTS SO MUCH YOU WOULD SWEAR YOU'VE BEEN LIFTING APPLIANCES IN YOUR SLEEP.

3. YOU JUST HAD AN INTERNAL EXAM, AND THE DOCTOR TOLD YOU WHAT COLOUR THE BABY'S HAIR IS. (JUST KIDDING THERE, BEST FRIEND, BUT HE OR SHE MIGHT HAVE TOLD YOU THAT YOU ARE TWO OR THREE CENTIMETRES DILATED AND COMPLETELY EFFACED.)

2. YOU ARE EXPERIENCING PERIOD-LIKE PAINS SO COMPELLING THAT YOU NOT ONLY CAN'T TALK DURING ONE, BUT YOU CAN'T LISTEN EITHER AND YOU THREATEN TO KILL ANYONE WHO CHATTERS TO YOU WHILE YOU QUAKE.

1. YOU ARE IN A HOSPITAL BED WATCHING *WHEEL OF FORTUNE* WITH AN INTRAVENOUS DRIP OF LABOUR-INDUCING PITOCIN* FLOWING THROUGH YOUR VEINS AND AN EPIDURAL COMFORTABLY NUMBING YOU FROM THE WAIST DOWN.

* Syntocin.

DATE --------------

Welcome to Maternity Limbo! From this time on, you are living in suspended animation. You're probably sick of being pregnant and exhausted from lack of sleep and surplus weight. We all agree that this 'holding pattern' is nearly unbearable. Don't be shocked if you feel even shorter-tempered than usual or cry several times a day.

You will make it, Best Friend, we promise. Try a thousand-piece jigsaw puzzle or put loose photos in your albums to distract yourself.

Notes

DATE _____

If your car is equipped with a passenger airbag, always put the baby's car seat (and the baby, too, when it comes) in the backseat. It doesn't take too great an impact to activate the bag, and the explosion upon opening can seriously hurt a tiny person.

Notes

_____

_____

_____

_____

_____

_____

DATE _____

Just when you thought you couldn't possibly look more pregnant, you grew some more. At this point, your belly is no longer a smooth, rounded protrusion, but something that seems to have points and corners where the elbows, feet and knees stick out. When a pregnant belly looks low and 'squared', you are approaching lift-off.

Notes

_____

_____

_____

_____

_____

_____

DATE ــــــــــــــ

Which mementos of your baby's birth should you save for posterity?
Certainly, you must keep the hospital bracelets that the two of you wore,
and the pink or blue name cards from the hospital crib. Lots of us save
the baby blanket with the name of the industrial laundry company on it,
and a really big favourite is the knitted cap they might give you if your
baby needs forceps, or has a hair wash in hospital.

More controversial is the belly button stump. We suggest that for
preserved body parts, you draw the line at locks of hair and baby teeth.

Notes

ـــ

ـــ

ـــ

ـــ

ـــ

ـــ

DATE _____

No matter how desperate you may be for distraction at this point, don't plan any weekend getaways. Even though you swear this baby is never coming, it is, and it wants to come to a hospital that it knows and trusts . . . not to the first-aid centre in Caesar's Palace. Stay within a forty-mile radius of the hospital where you are booked.

NOTES

_____

_____

_____

_____

_____

_____

DATE _____

Beg, bribe or call your MP to make sure that you will be able to stay in the hospital for at least 48 hours after delivery. Sure, the food stinks and the pillows are made out of packing materials, but it's filled with doctors and nurses and other people who are sure to know much more about new babies than you do. One of this Best Friend's most treasured memories was in the middle of the night in the hospital, watching old movies with her brand-new baby. Sheer bliss, especially if someone happens to send you a congratulatory muffin or biscuit basket.

Notes

_____

_____

_____

_____

_____

_____

DATE _____

When you feel like your spine just can't take this pregnancy one more minute, get down on your hands and knees – not to pray, although it couldn't hurt – but to do what are called 'cat stretches'. First, slowly curve your back up like a scared cat, then gently release it into a swayback. Do this five or ten times to get a little blood circulating. Then, feel free to lie down on the floor and take a nap.

Notes

_____

_____

_____

_____

_____

_____

DATE --------------

To snip or not to snip. If you have a boy, you will be asked, before your baby is 24 hours old, whether you intend to circumcise him. A practice that has been routine in the US for years is now being reexamined. Most mothers are tempted to take the route of the least amount of discomfort, but most fathers assume that their son's penis must look exactly like their penis.

We suggest you let your partner make this call since penis care is not within our immediate area of expertise, and, if you are Jewish, there really is no use in questioning the divine wisdom of God and men. Women used to get burned at the stake for far less.

Notes

DATE _____

At this point, it musl seem to you that you visit the clinic every other day. They really start paying attention when you're this pregnant.

Try to be bathed and groomed for every one of these visits because if you can't pull it together for your midwife, you have really lost your grip. Besides, the other people in the clinic are looking to you for inspiration, not to be terrified by impending motherhood.

Notes

_____

_____

_____

_____

_____

_____

DATE _____

If you have already received baby gifts, write your thank-you notes
TODAY. You will receive more gifts after the baby is born, and if you get
behind now, you will never catch up. Remember, it
will seem like only moments before you're writing
thank-yous for the holidays, and before you know
it, first birthdays are here with more gifts to be
acknowledged.

Notes

_____

_____

_____

_____

_____

_____

THIRD TRIMESTER   18 DAYS TO GO

DATE _____

You will be overwhelmed by many, many things in the weeks to come, and one of the important lessons for you to start teaching your partner is that he will be responsible for various things in the near future that normally he would expect you to handle. But you'll have your hands full, literally and figuratively.

P.S. Among the new daddy jobs will be helping you with thank-yous for gifts and flowers and manning the phones. (He does handle a full-time job; he should be able to swing this.)

NOTES

DATE _ _ _ _ _ _ _ _ _ _ _ _ _

Is there petrol in the car?

Never let the tank get below half-empty from now until your children are married and gone. Trust us, you will not want to stop for a fill-up when you're in labour, nor will you in the future when you are driving a vomiting six-year-old to the doctor's.

Notes

_____

_____

_____

_____

_____

_____

DATE _____

You will have a bloody discharge for weeks after delivery, whether it was a vaginal or caesarean birth. I considered investing in a sanitary pad company (remember, you won't be using tampons yet) because, in the beginning, I was using two or three at a time. The flow will change colour, from reddish to brownish to yellowish to gone. If you notice blood that looks like what comes out of a cut, rather than menstrual-looking blood, call the doctor; you might be haemorrhaging.

NOTES

_____

_____

_____

_____

_____

_____

DATE _____

It's never too early to obsess ahead; you will be completely within your rights to demand that all visitors, even your partner should you deem it necessary, wash with antibacterial soap before entering your baby's universe. Some mums feel that even this is not enough protection (you can't help yourself), and they require guests to wear surgical gowns or drape themselves in a large baby blanket. You are the boss here. You have the right to dip them in hydrogen peroxide as far as we are concerned, since there is absolutely no use in trying to act rationally at such a fragile time as this.

NOTES

_____

_____

_____

_____

_____

_____

DATE _____

Sometime in the next few weeks, you will ask yourself, 'If the species has relied on breastfeeding for survival all these millennia, why is it so hard to learn?' You would think nothing would be more natural than putting a baby to your breast and having it feed until satisfied, but that seldom happens. Instead, the mum and the baby both often end up in tears before a successful 'docking manoeuvre', because latching on is more complex than a lunar landing.

NOTES

_____

_____

_____

_____

_____

_____

DATE _____

Brand-new babies do not look like the kids in the nappy commercials.
Newborns usually look skinny and much smaller than you imagined a
human being could be. They also sometimes have downy fur on their
shoulders and back. (Don't worry, this disappears soon and remains
dormant until the baby turns into a middle-aged man who insists on
wearing a muscle T-shirt.) New babies often have complexion problems of
their own. Little white spots can cluster around the nose and chin. Don't
fuss over these minor imperfections . . . the world will still recognize that
your precious one is just as beautiful as you and Daddy think it is.

NOTES

_____

_____

_____

_____

_____

_____

DATE _____

Trust me when I tell you BREASTFEEDING DOES NOT PROTECT YOU FROM GETTING PREGNANT!!! If you lose your mind and have sex as soon as a few days after delivery, you can conceive again. You must use birth control unless you find the idea of two babies under a year old appealing. If you breastfeed, you will be advised to choose some form of birth control other than the traditional pill, probably one with reduced oestrogen.

NOTES

DATE _____

Get ready for company because new babies draw visitors like a magnet. You are entitled to request no visitors for the first week or two, but after that, people are going to think you are hiding something from them.

Do not feel obliged to clean the house for guests, nor are you expected to offer anything more than a glass of tap water . . . no matter what your mother says.

Notes

_____

_____

_____

_____

_____

_____

DATE _____

Make sure that you have enough groceries to last for a couple of weeks.

Sure, you can ask someone to pick up milk or fruit for you while you're housebound, but you won't want to reach for toilet paper, sanitary pads or nappies in the middle of the night only to find you have run out.

Notes

_____

_____

_____

_____

_____

_____

DATE --------------

If you haven't already bought your baby's car seat, get it today. If you already have it, spend some time before the baby comes reading the directions. Use a teddy bear as your surrogate baby to practise putting the harness over its wobbly head and releasing the infant carrier from the base that is fastened to the car with a seat belt. The time to learn these manoeuvres, which are harder than they look to the uninitiated, is now – not when the baby is crying and you are approaching hysteria.

Remember,

BABY CAR SEATS MUST FACE THE REAR OF THE CAR.

Notes

DATE _____

If you don't already have a phonecard, get one now. You can buy them in specific credit amounts and use them until you've yakked to their maximum. This is really more a gift for your partner so that he won't have to come to the hospital with pockets jingling full of change for the pay phones. He will have a lot of calls to make when the baby is born, and he might not want to use the phone in your room, if there is one, because you're sleeping.

NoteS

_____

_____

_____

_____

_____

_____

DATE --------------

Understand right now that the only way to know for certain that you're in labour is for someone, preferably someone medically trained, to look inside you and see if you're opening up. That means that you are not expected to be able to make that determination yourself. Never, ever, ever be embarrassed if you go to the hospital or call your midwife only to be told that you still have some more waiting to do. You deserve extra attention right now, whether the baby is coming out or not. We promise, no one will be mad at you if you get fooled by those nasty old Braxton Hicks contractions, because they fool nearly everyone.

NOTES

THIRD TRIMESTER 6 DAYS TO GO

DATE _____

Make sure that you have infant Calpol and an infant thermometer in the house before you bring the baby home from the hospital. These two things are more important than almost any other baby paraphernalia because you will want to know if your little one has a temperature and be able to bring it down.*

Rectal thermometers give a more accurate reading, but they can be terrifying to a new mum. If you simply can't buy one of those new electronic ear thermometers right now, and no one has given you one as an incredibly generous gift, insist that a nurse teach you how to take a rectal temperature before you leave the hospital.

* Most doctors and health visitors do not advise giving a baby under three months Calpol, unless on their say-so.

NOTES

_____

_____

_____

_____

DATE _____

If you have been enjoying the long, strong fingernails of pregnancy for the last nine (ten) months, you might want to consider getting a sensible mummy manicure now. Most of us feel like we are all thumbs when taking care of newborns anyway, and when those thumbs have daggers on their tips, you risk scratching or poking the baby. Cut them down to fingertip length and just put a coat of clear polish on them since you won't have time to maintain those Joan Crawford talons anymore.

Notes

_____

_____

_____

_____

_____

_____

DATE _____

While this is not a La Leche League ad, and we don't ultimately have the
right to dictate whether you should breastfeed or not, here is one thing to
consider: breastfeeding forces us to cut out the meaningless business of
our lives and pay attention to the baby and ourselves. One of our greatest
mistakes as mothers these days is to rush our recovery from pregnancy
and childbirth. Breastfeeding can force us overachievers to prioritize our
lives properly to make room for the addition to the family, rather than
darting off to gym classes or throwing ourselves back into our careers.

NOTES

DATE   _____

Here's the Ultimate Best Friends Tip: the minute you enter the hospital start asking for an *epidural* (a combination of drugs released into the fluid surrounding your spinal cord through a needle, by an anaesthetist, in your lower back) and continue until you receive one. Labour is not a contest, you don't win anything by going painkiller-free and if you think you want to go au naturel, talk to me afterwards.

Notes

_____

_____

_____

_____

_____

_____

DATE _____   *OverDue!*

Has your due date come and gone without incident? Don't be too disappointed . . . it really is a toss of the coin, since half of the pregnant population will deliver 'early' and the other half will deliver 'late'.

Here's a suggestion: beg your partner to have passionate, penetrative sex with you tonight. His semen has oxytocin in it, the chemical that brings on contractions. Even if you don't go into labour, you'll have killed some time in a pleasant fashion.

Notes

_____

_____

_____

_____

_____

_____

DATE _ _ _ _ _ _ _ _ _ _ _ _ _

Still no baby? Trust us when we say, emphatically, that a baby in your belly is easier to take care of than one outside your belly.

Try to rest and, by all means, take your phone off the hook. There is nothing more tedious than having to tell twenty callers a day that no, the baby isn't here yet.

Haul yourself outside for as brisk a walk as you can muster. Walking forces the baby's head gently against your cervix, and it might get things moving in there.

Notes

_____

_____

_____

_____

_____

_____

SEE YOU AFTERWARDS,
WHENEVER THAT IS!

HAPPY LABOUR DAY

DATE _____

My sister-in-law pushed so hard during delivery that afterwards, the whites of her eyes turned red. Several of my other Best Friends noticed broken capillaries on their cheeks. We've even met women who bruised under their eyes while getting that baby out. I just wanted to be the first to tell you a delivery horror story!

Even if none of these things happens to you, you will almost certainly find your face swollen and your eyes puffy a few hours after giving birth. Ask the midwife for two ice packs, one to put on your face and one to put between your legs.

Notes

_____

_____

_____

_____

_____

_____

DATE _____

You may have noticed your doctor sucking fluids out of your baby's nose with a rubber bulb before the little thing has even got all the way out of your body.* Make sure you don't leave the hospital without one or two of those nose suckers.

Babies haven't mastered the art of sniffling, let alone blowing their nose. You can offer a lot of relief by sticking the bulb in those itsy-bitsy nostrils, and giving them one good suck.

Babies generally hate it, but us mums love them almost as much as we love cottonbuds.

* Not routine in the UK.

Notes

_____

_____

_____

_____

_____

DATE _____

Unbelievable, isn't it? They will actually trust you enough to send the baby home in your care. It's ten times harder to rent a car, even a mini! The people at the hospital know something you don't: that no one on this planet can care for this little darling better than its mum.

notes

_____

_____

_____

_____

_____

_____

DATE _____

What with episiotomy stitches, haemorrhoids and the general wear and tear of delivery, you must be looking forward to your first bowel movement with the same uncontainable excitement of someone facing dental surgery. Suddenly you have pushing flashbacks and you are filled with dread. Unless you prefer being full of you-know-what, you have no choice but to march into that bathroom and eliminate! Yes, it hurts, but nothing tears or breaks, contrary to the vivid sensations.

NOTES

_____

_____

_____

_____

_____

_____

DATE _____

Take a moment to really look at your baby's ears. Paediatricians maintain that the ear is the last bit of physical development (along with the lung membranes) to develop on a foetus, so to really feel the miracle of this little being, take a look at the ears . . . so tiny, and yet there they are with little lobes, curves and folds. If your baby was born prematurely, the ears will develop the same, but it will happen on the outside where you can watch it. Everyone talks about the relief of finding ten toes and fingers, but those ears should at least get equal time.

NOTES

_____

_____

_____

_____

_____

_____

DATE _____

Protecting your baby from germs is critical in the first few weeks when its immune system is just warming up, but many mothers can be obsessed with very little prodding. A dummy dropped on the floor doesn't really need to be destroyed . . . boiling water would satisfy even Jonas Salk. A surgical mask on visitors is rarely called for unless they are spewing phlegm or have open sores, in which case they shouldn't be in your neighbourhood, let alone holding your child. Even a good wet kiss from the family dog will probably do little harm, so keep the dog and try not to let it drink out of toilets.

NOTES

_____
_____
_____
_____
_____
_____

DATE _____

Try lying on your tummy for the first time in ages. Roll over slowly
because your insides are still sore and out of alignment, and put a soft
pillow under your breasts, which may be filling with milk.

Doesn't that feel amazing? For the first time in ages, you can feel the
separate vertebrae in your spine rather than the sensation that the whole
apparatus was fused into wrought iron months ago.

If you have had a caesarean, wait a few more days, and put a pillow
against your incision before you enjoy this simple pleasure.

NOTES

_____

_____

_____

_____

_____

_____

DATE _____

If your birth experience was complicated and not what you dreamed it would be, it is very likely that you feel sadness, resentment and maybe even guilt. Some women who ended up with unexpected caesareans still mourn years later that they didn't get the birth they had planned and prepared for. There is a faint inkling that they have failed at something that should have come so naturally to them.

Get over it! You did the right thing, at great sacrifice to yourself, and the truth of that lies in the baby in your arms. But you still need to believe it yourself.

NOTES

_____

_____

_____

_____

_____

_____

DATE _____

During the week or two following delivery, you are likely to wake up in the middle of the night so wet that you swear someone hosed you down. This is just nature's way of helping you get rid of all the water you have been retaining. Sleep on towels until the sauna stage passes, and never sleep in silky lingerie (as if!) because it just gets cold and sticky when wet. It's a drag to wake up and find yourself drowning, but it does lead to weight loss, and that's what counts.

Notes

_____

_____

_____

_____

_____

_____

DATE _____

It can be several days, even weeks, before you will be able to stand for more than a minute without having the sensation that your uterus is so heavy that it is going to fall out of your body and land with a splat on the bathroom floor.

Remember that pelvic floor area that you could never identify when you tried out exercises? Well, guess what? You've found it! See, I wasn't just haranguing you when I told you to keep up the pelvic-floor exercises. Start again today, and continue until you are so old that you don't mind wearing a nappy every day.

NOTES

DATE _____

Babies aren't supposed to be bathed until their belly button stumps fall off. I only mention it now because I completely forgot this rule when my fourth baby was born (so much for practice-makes-perfect). As cute as 'Baby's First Bath' photos and videos are, there is no good reason to rush into the total body plunge. A wet and sudsy baby is harder to hold on to than a live trout.

Stick with the sponge bathing until your best mum friend or one of the grandmas come by to spot you. You will also need a third adult in the room, perhaps Daddy, to operate the cameras.

Notes

_____

_____

_____

_____

_____

_____

DATE _____   *Relax & Nap*

Wow, time flies when you're physically and mentally exhausted. Welcome to the real world of motherhood. We're here to help you through the next couple of months, and our first pearls of wisdom? Hook up the answering machine (always screen calls until further notice) and take a nap.

Notes

_____

_____

_____

_____

_____

_____

DATE _____

You, too, should avoid tub baths until your midwife or health visitor tells you otherwise. Until your cervix closes up nice and tight again, you run the risk of introducing bacteria (not to mention bubble bath) into your uterus. If you need to relieve your stitches and/or haemorrhoids, go ahead and sit in three to four inches of hot water (otherwise known as a sitz bath), but don't recline (as if you had the time).

Notes

_____

_____

_____

_____

_____

_____

DATE _____

New mums are often alarmed at the cramps they feel during breastfeeding. They can actually be painful, but this is usually more common with second or third babies.

This sensation is no cause for alarm (at least no more alarming than the countless other excretions, bruises, stitches and herniated tissue that you've already faced). In fact, it is a good thing because it means your uterus is tightening back up to its prepregnancy size of a pear.

NOTES

_____

_____

_____

_____

_____

_____

DATE _ _ _ _ _ _ _ _ _ _ _ _ _

Don't be concerned by the appearance of your precious baby's belly
button. Sure, you were probably alarmed by how big and dark it looked,
but fear not, because how it looks in the first few weeks has no bearing
on whether it will ultimately end up an 'inny' or an 'outy'. Your job at this
time is to protect it while the stump is healing and to keep it clean (which
takes tremendous intestinal fortitude since we are all afraid to go digging
around in there with our swabs).

Notes

_____

_____

_____

_____

_____

_____

DATE _____

Baby immunizations are unbearably painful; not for the baby, but for YOU! You know it's time for that first inoculation, and since you're the grown-up here, you must take your baby in for its first brush with a needle.* Buck up, Best Friend, you'll make that doctor's appointment and you'll keep it. Most importantly, you will be there holding your baby in your arms and perhaps offering it a little nip at the breast for comfort. The little darling will forget about this travesty by the time you tuck it back into its car seat, even if you are still sobbing uncontrollably an hour later.

Mummyhood is not for wimps!

* The first of the three DTP vaccinations is usually at two months in the UK.

Notes

_____

_____

_____

_____

_____

DATE _____

The first couple of weeks (at least) of breastfeeding can be really painful. Our soft nipples will balk at having someone sucking on them constantly. And let's talk about how hard a baby that size can suck! Now's the time for those Lamaze breathing techniques.

By the way, if you had always planned to breastfeed, don't let this agony be the reason you stop. Try to stick it out one more week. Breastfeeding not only becomes absolutely painless, but the uterine contractions that go along with it actually start feeling vaguely reminiscent of orgasm. Swear to God!

NOtes

_____

_____

_____

_____

_____

_____

DATE _____

Nipples that are cracked and scabbed will not get better by being rubbed with various creams. Just keep on breastfeeding; the baby won't notice how raggedy you look or feel. The only cure is to break on through to the other side.

When you aren't feeding, take every opportunity to expose your nipples to air. Keep your bra flaps open after you've finished feeding to let them dry. It's really quite a sight for someone who accidentally walks in on you at this time. There is little more you can do for the poor darlings, except perhaps send them on a vacation for two to St Bart's.

NOTES

_____
_____
_____
_____
_____
_____

DATE _____

H2O

Have you heard the old folk advice to drink beer to stimulate your milk production? I'm no teetotaller, but this suggestion sounds like a hackneyed excuse (completely understandable, however) to take a nip now and then to dull the latch-on pain. Other than anaesthesia, there is little beer contributes that you can't get from a big glass of water. Remember that ultimately, alcohol is a diuretic and will dry you out.

There, end of sermon.

Notes

_____

_____

_____

_____

_____

_____

DATE _____

Speaking of water, never sit down to breastfeed without a huge glass or bottle of water right beside you. As soon as the baby latches on, your mouth will get so dry that your tongue sticks to the roof. Isn't Mother Nature clever to remind you in such a vivid way that the milk factory relies on a steady infusion of water?

Keep bottles of water in all the places where you used to keep antacids. Go to sleep at night with a big glass of ice, so the middle-of-the-night feed finds you with something remotely cold.

Notes

_____

_____

_____

_____

_____

_____

DATE _____

Time to pick up the electric breast pump you reserved. The places that rent these pumps are generally staffed by women who know volumes about babies, breastfeeding and pumping, so plan to spend some time with them learning everything you can. The highlight of the orientation is when you are shown how to pump both breasts at the same time! Old Bossy the Cow has nothing on you, Best Friend!

NOTES

_____

_____

_____

_____

_____

_____

DATE _____

Is your baby becoming a tyrant? Sure, he fooled you those first couple of weeks; all he did was sleep, eat and daintily dirty a nappy now and then. Now he is crying at all hours, particularly near dinnertime when you are most crushingly exhausted, and you are going crazy with your inability to find the cause of his misery and cure it.

Guess what, even as we enter the millennium, no one is really sure what makes babies fussy or colicky. We only know that this, too, shall pass – usually by the time the baby is three months old. Hold on, Best Friend!

NOTES

_____

_____

_____

_____

_____

_____

DATE _____

If you are secretly beginning to feel a bit resentful of your baby's seemingly endless demands, if you have walked up and down the hall till you've worn a path in the carpet, breastfed so much that you haven't closed your bra flaps in two days and if you can't remember the last time you slept long enough to dream, it's time to reach out for help. Trust us, since we are undoubtedly thinking more clearly than you are at this point, all good mums know when to take a break so that they can come back to their mothering tasks with a better outlook and new vitality. Get a babysitter, a partner, or any pair of loving arms to cover for you, and take a break.

NOTES

_____

_____

_____

_____

_____

_____

BABY SISSORS

DATE _____

Babies' fingernails are like switchblades, and they can easily scratch the little beauty's face. This presents yet another Mummy Nightmare. It is so easy to cut the nails too short or to nick the baby's soft fingertips. OK, I confess, I cut my son's nails so short that he lost the top layer of his thumb.

1. Cut the nails with baby *scissors* rather than little *clippers*.

2. Attempt all manicures when the baby is sleeping. We all know it's impossible to hit a moving target.

3. When all else fails, bite the nails off with your own teeth.

Notes

_____

_____

_____

_____

_____

_____

DATE _____

News flash! Your baby will continue to breathe even when you are not staring at it and willing it to do so. Don't worry, we all have tried to stay awake and vigilant day and night when we brought our tiny little babies home from the hospital, but fatigue eventually strikes down even the most neurotic of us. You must rest. It helps ease some anxiety if you keep the baby in a crib beside your bed or if you put the baby monitor in the cot beside the baby so that you can hear every delicious breath it takes. Now, go lie down.

NOTES

DATE   _____

If you are breastfeeding, remember to keep your feet up. It's also a good idea to put a cushion or pillow in your lap. The idea here is to bring Mohammed closer to the Mountain. If the baby is up near your nipple, you will have less of a tendency to support her with your arms, a technique that invariably leads to 'nursing neck' – a painful stiffness that comes from hours of sitting with your shoulders scrunched while your baby eats.

If anyone asks if you need help, get him to massage your neck and shoulders.

NOtes

_____

_____

_____

_____

_____

_____

DATE _____

A baby monitor takes some getting used to. First of all, you will be tempted to turn the volume up so high that you will not only hear every whimper, but the sound of the baby's hair growing! Then, when he gives one good cry, you will sustain more hearing damage than a teenager at a rave.

A word of warning: baby noises are not the only sounds that monitors relay. I know of a father who used the private phone in the nanny's room to set up a tryst while his wife heard the entire illicit conversation over the baby monitor. She has custody, and he has occasional visitation.

Notes

_____

_____

_____

_____

_____

_____

DATE _____

Don't think your partner has become some sort of deviant just because he expresses interest in what your breast milk tastes like. The simple answer is, it tastes rather like coconut milk, and is sort of watery and very sweet.

Chances are, however, he is really more interested in trying out the whole breastfeeding experience. Our advice is, once your nipples have toughened up and no longer hurt, go ahead and give him a little sip. Later, when you find yourself engorged with milk and without a hungry baby or a breast pump nearby, your partner's willingness to suck may be all that stands between you and an explosion.

NOTES

_____

_____

_____

_____

_____

_____

DATE _____

Let's talk about sex again. Aside from your first post-delivery bowel movement, few things are more terrifying than the thought of your partner (or even Mel Gibson, for that matter) penetrating your poor, traumatized privates. Sure, you sympathize with his begging and pleading, but don't make any unnecessary sacrifices. And when the magic moment arrives, make sure that you're on top so that you can control the speed and accuracy.

P.S. See Day 38!

Notes

_____

_____

_____

_____

_____

_____

DATE _____

Breastfeeding in public is a touchy subject. Sooner or later you WILL have to do it, in spite of all plans to the contrary, so here are your options:

You can buy those funny button-front flap shirts that hide your breasts and make it look like you're holding a headless baby. You can cape yourself and the baby with a big receiving blanket, creating a sort of tent for the two of you wherever you are. Or, you can simply whip it out, the breast, I mean, and glare at anyone who gives you the hairy eyeball. Pride always fails before a hungry baby's cry.

NOTES

DATE _____

Right about now, you might be quite certain that one child is enough for any family. Who in her right mind would spend another year going through this again, right? There's an old cliché that says, 'If it was men who did the birthin', every kid would be an only child.'

While this baby's birth may, indeed, complete your family perfectly, most of you will eventually be willing to go back for more. This is not because we women are inherently more courageous than men (although we are), but rather because motherhood causes brain damage and impairs judgement.

Notes

_____

_____

_____

_____

_____

_____

DATE _____

If this is not your first baby, you must be awakening to the fact that no mother in the universe is capable of giving all the time and attention that she thinks each of her children needs and deserves. You are constantly torn between the new baby and your toddler who so clearly misses you.

Try to calm down about it now because it gets worse. Just wait until you go back to work or return to the full responsibilities of running a home. Think of sibling rivalry as a *gift* to children to hone their social skills and inspire a healthy sense of competition. Whatever you do, don't reveal your frustration to your kids because they have no compassion and will use that information against you later in therapy.

NOTES

DATE _____

If you are breastfeeding and eventually plan on weaning your child before he can ask for fries with that shake, it's never too early to introduce the bottle. The longer he goes without it, the harder it will be to adapt later. When you do try the bottle, have Daddy give it at the end of the day so you can get some extra hours of uninterrupted sleep and your partner can not only do some bonding, he can put the baby to bed.

Notes

_____

_____

_____

_____

_____

_____

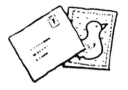

DATE _____

If you have the time and energy, go ahead and send birth announcements to everyone you know. Sure, they can be perceived as a thinly veiled request for gifts, but, hey, no one is twisting those cynics' arms! This is the way the Best Friends see it: the birth of a baby is a miracle and should be heralded as such. If you can arrange for the Star of Bethlehem to shine over your nursery, why not?

Notes

_____

_____

_____

_____

_____

_____

DATE ---------------

Here's our twopen'orth on the subject of godparents. If you are of a faith that has a tradition of naming godparents, we think you should try to pick blood relatives.

In this transient day, your best friend from college and your partner's boss may ultimately not be there for the baby in the long run. Relatives, no matter how you feel about them, do tend to stick around.

NOtes

36

DATE _____

How can we put this to you gently? Leggings, thick socks with dirty soles, a giant T-shirt and a dressing gown adorning an unwashed, unshaved body can actually turn some men off. Remember, now is not the time to lose your partner intentionally, because it's hard to find a replacement when your breasts are still leaking and you have fifteen extra pounds glued to you (and that's BEFORE you pick up the baby!).

NOTES

_____

_____

_____

_____

_____

_____

DATE _____

Check on the status of the baby's birth certificate. You may have sent in the paperwork from the hospital, but many of us end up taking home handfuls of paperwork, and one of those scraps is probably the birth certificate form. Until you get the official certificate from the state, you will most likely have a semi-official certificate from the hospital to prove that you have, indeed, had a baby, not a hallucination.*

* In the UK you must register the birth before the baby is six weeks old. The Register Office number is in the phone book.

Notes

_____

_____

_____

_____

_____

DATE _____

It's about time for your six-week postnatal checkup. Assuming everything down there has healed and shrunk back to a recognizable size, you will be given the green light to have full-tilt sex (as distinguished from satisfying his 'needs' through methods that are still illegal in some Southern states).

BEST FRIENDS UNITE! DO NOT SHARE THE DOCTOR'S 'BLESSING' WITH YOUR PARTNER UNTIL YOU FEEL READY. THE FICTION OF THE SIX-WEEK RECOVERY IS THE RESULT OF A MALE CONSPIRACY!

NOTES

_____

_____

_____

_____

_____

_____

DATE _____

More than half of us new mums have to face the prospect of going back to work soon, and we all know how traumatic it feels.

Your attention should be focused on arranging who will care for your baby while you are at work, and how to juggle your schedule a bit to sneak some baby time in. It's a tough adjustment, since instinct tells us to keep that baby near us at all times . . . but millions of us have done it, and so can you.

Notes

_____

_____

_____

_____

_____

_____

DATE _____

Those of you who only have a six-week maternity leave from work* should start preparing for your return now. There are three major concerns:

1. Putting together a presentable wardrobe. Take a look at the things you wore when you were about five months pregnant.

2. Learning to pump your breast milk or beginning to wean your baby on to formula.

3. Trying not to sob any time you think about spending an entire day without your baby. It's like the first day of nursery . . . you cry and mope the entire day, but pretty soon, you realize that seeing all the other kids at school is kind of fun.

* You are entitled to 14 weeks' leave, but only receive higher rate SMP for six weeks.

NOTES

_____

_____

_____

_____

DATE _____

A little tired during that 3 A.M. feeding?

Bring the baby to bed and breastfeed until someone falls asleep, partners not included. Don't worry, nobody will roll over on the baby in the middle of the night.

Hard to believe, isn't it? Check with your doctor, he or she will assure you that it's perfectly safe.

Notes

_____

_____

_____

_____

_____

_____

DATE _____

Here you are, back at work, looking pretty good and having fun seeing the old gang again.

Then all of a sudden it hits you: you have left your precious baby in the care of someone you hardly know and pay £200 a week! They can easily make £10,000 selling your perfect angel on the black market! What were you thinking?

Here's what you were thinking: you did your homework and selected the best person you could find to care for your baby. She is sweet and nurturing, she has references, and besides, you've hidden a video camera on the bookshelf to monitor her every move.

NOTES

DATE --------------

Lots of new mums worry that their baby likes the nanny or housekeeper more than them. Relax, your baby still thinks it is you. Sure, maybe the more experienced care of the nanny (who has done this before) may be more calming to the baby, but that doesn't mean it doesn't love you more than heaven and earth. It probably just means that you smell like milk and when you hold the baby, it thinks it's chow time. In a few months, you will have more obvious evidence that you are the centre of your baby's universe . . . like when you have to sneak out of the house to avoid an awful separation scene.

Notes

DATE _ _ _ _ _ _ _ _ _ _ _ _ _

Are three balanced meals a day not on the top of your priority list? For the baby's sake you really need your strength, especially if you're breastfeeding and you're responsible for all her nutritional needs. Wait until she's toilet-trained before she exists on a diet of fast food. But let's not jump ahead.

Now is not the time to be dieting. Don't you remember? Nine (ten) months up, nine (ten) months down.

P.S. How are those pelvic-floor exercises coming along?

NoteS

_____

_____

_____

_____

_____

DATE _ _ _ _ _ _ _ _ _ _ _ _ _ _

Is your partner feeling left out? This is a time when it is particularly difficult to drag your attention from your enchanting little baby to focus on bathing yourself, let alone noticing your poor partner. Try to remember that he used to be your baby and now he feels like an orphan, so a little petulance is understandable . . . not necessarily curable, but understandable.

Notes

_____

_____

_____

_____

_____

_____

FOURTH TRIMESTER   DAY 46 OF MOTHERHOOD

DATE   _____

Start asking around for baby-sitters. I know the thought of leaving your precious child with a gum-snapping Spice Girls fanatic sounds unthinkable, but there will come a time when you and your partner will want to get out for at least the first half of a movie, and it is imperative that you learn to trust someone (well, trust may be too strong a word) or take a chance on someone besides yourself being able to care for your child.

Good luck. Our prayers are with you.

Notes

_____

_____

_____

_____

_____

_____

DATE _____

Ready for the big date? Is it about time to resume 'full marital relations' with your partner? Keep two words in mind: inebriate and lubricate.

A glass of red wine (think goblet-size) does wonders to relax you and make you feel amorous.

It also helps you forget your terror that your vagina is going to be ripped to shreds. You will need the lubrication because you will be dry, dry, dry down there, no matter how aroused you feel. Other than that, remind your partner to be gentle and proceed more slowly than his horniness would have him go. You'll have fun, even if your orgasm machine is still out of whack.

NOTES

_____

_____

_____

_____

_____

DATE _____

You may already have discovered accidentally what we're going to tell you now. The loud, droning sound of certain appliances, such as vacuums, blenders and hair-dryers, puts lots of babies right to sleep. When you have some steam to blow or the baby just won't stop howling, consider putting the baby in a front pack and vacuuming the house. Feel free to yell or sing because you just blend in with the noise. The baby will be snoozing.

NOTES

_____

_____

_____

_____

_____

_____

DATE _____

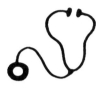

Remember how we told you to make good use of
your midwife, with questions and phone calls? Well,
the same holds true for your GP. If you're not happy
with the practice then move on. There are no rules
that you have to stick it out with that doctor. The only
one you have to stick it out with is your baby.

Notes

_____

_____

_____

_____

_____

_____

DATE _ _ _ _ _ _ _ _ _ _ _

If you are working outside the home and the baby is not with you, try not to get into too many conversations about your little angel. The more vividly and lovingly you describe him or her, the more apt you are to feel a longing. The more longing you feel, the greater the chance that your letdown reflex will occur and you will look like an also-ran in a wet T-shirt contest.

NotES

_____

_____

_____

_____

_____

_____

DATE _____

It's time to learn the motherly art of the 'little white lie'. Our society and especially our employers just don't seem to understand the importance of being there for the critical life passages of our babies. Sure, you can be honest and tell everyone that you are leaving work early, with that important deal incomplete, because your baby is getting a shot, but you won't be respected for it. You must create a non-maternal excuse, such as a sales call or a meeting outside the office.

Notes

_____

_____

_____

_____

_____

_____

DATE _____

We all know that solitary confinement is one of the highest forms of punishment in our penal system. Well, add a crying baby to that and you have motherhood on a really bad day. Isolation can be a real problem for new mums. Rather than attack your partner each evening, starving for conversation, pack up the baby every day and get out of the house. That's what 'mother and baby' groups are for.

NOtes

_____

_____

_____

_____

_____

_____

DATE _____

Postnatal depression is real and probably touches all of us new mums to varying degrees, whether we recognize it or not. It is not a sign of failure, nor is it imagined. It is also not a silly little case of tears a couple of days after giving birth, as some books would have you believe. It is the lethal combination of hormonal havoc, exhaustion, isolation and irrevocable change. If you think you have it, call your doctor today, because you can be helped.

NOTES

_____

_____

_____

_____

_____

_____

DATE _____

Don't you love the smell of your baby? Do you know that a study was
done where brand-new mums were blindfolded and asked to pick out
their baby from a group of several newborns based only on smell? The
mothers were able to pick almost every time. Isn't nature grand?

Notes

_____

_____

_____

_____

_____

_____

DATE --------------

Is this motherhood business a lot different from what you fantasized when you were still pregnant? Funny how that works, isn't it? Those women in formula commercials singing to their babies while walking on the beach really piss us off.

That 'mum' isn't sleep-deprived, thrown up on, or experiencing postnatal pimples.

She probably isn't even really a mum.

NoteS

DATE _____

Even the most finicky and organized of us lose all control of our
environment when a new baby comes home to live with us. You will
wonder, as you step over piles of laundry in every room of the house, how
one tiny baby can require so much time and work. Once again, we
remind you: pregnancy and motherhood are lessons in surrender.

NOTES

DATE _____

It goes without saying that your partner isn't as good at baby care as you are. You have two choices, as you watch him fling his hand around madly trying to get the nappy tab unstuck from his fingers while keeping the other hand on the baby so he doesn't escape, only to have him pee in his face:

1. You can tell him he's inept and complete the task in your own perfect way, or

2. You can let him struggle through on the assumption that practice makes passable and let him know that he better get the hang of it.

Notes

_____

_____

_____

_____

_____

_____

DATE _ _ _ _ _ _ _ _ _ _ _ _

Have you just found yourself with a moment of calm? Wouldn't having a cup of tea and watching 'Neighbours' feel great right now? Sorry, it's time for you to write a few thank-you notes for the baby gifts that seem to arrive on a daily basis. People really do sit around waiting for them, unless, of course, they, too, are mothers of small kids. Give your partner the job of posting them for you when he goes to work, since you won't find time to get to a post office to buy stamps for several more months, if ever.

Notes

_____

_____

_____

_____

_____

_____

DATE _____

Babies do not give you advance notice before they roll over for the first time. That means that you should expect it to happen at any time. Never, ever leave the baby on a changing table or bed for one moment because that will be the moment it hurls itself into the wild blue yonder.

Notes

_____

_____

_____

_____

_____

_____

DATE _____

Mother's intuition is very real and very reliable. Trust your instincts. If you think your baby is feeling sick, it probably is. If you think it hates wearing booties, you're probably right. There is some kind of extraordinary communication between a mother and child (at least until the teen years), and it will guide you in making the right parenting decisions most of the time.

NOTES

_____

_____

_____

_____

_____

_____

DATE _____

Do you secretly believe that no one, particularly your partner, can properly care for your baby? Sure, we want the dads to join in and share this parenting experience, but do we really *trust* them? Most of us hover around barking such observations as 'Don't drop her!' or 'Watch his neck!' or 'Any fool knows that the picture band goes on the *front* of the nappy!'

You're not helping here! Fatigue alone should soon cure you of this nagging.

NOTES

_____
_____
_____
_____
_____
_____

DATE _____

Go ahead and ask your partner the same question we all feel obliged to ask when having sex after birth: 'Does it feel the same down there?' If he is smart, he will lie and tell you it feels the same, if not better. Never ask again.

Notes

_____
_____
_____
_____
_____
_____

DATE _____

A lazy bladder is a legacy of pregnancy. Thousands of women who have had vaginal births cannot sneeze without wetting their pants. Others say they just can't 'hold it' like they used to. You may find yourself unable to sleep an entire night without getting up to use the bathroom. Look at it this way: a nocturnal stroll gives you a chance to go in and check on the baby.

NOTES

_____

_____

_____

_____

_____

_____

DATE _____

If you have a pretty good relationship to begin with, adding a baby to the mix just makes it better. Suddenly, you love your partner not just because he's sweet or cute or sexy . . . you love him because he loves your child. In years to come, you will almost ache with love for what a good daddy he is and how bonded the two of you are in your commitment to your family. Then, again, there will be times that you have the biggest fights of your life over differing parenting styles. *C'est la vie*!

NOtes

_____

_____

_____

_____

_____

_____

DATE _____

Never wake a sleeping baby. We know they look so delicious lying there asleep, their little mouths sleep-sucking, their little hands in fists under their chins, but don't pick them up! Feel free to look until the image is etched into your heart, but then you must go and rest for a few minutes. This opportunity will not last forever.

NOTES

DATE _____

Baby swings can be emancipation for new mums. As you well know, babies prefer gentle movement to being still, but that movement does not necessarily have to be provided exclusively by you. Borrow or buy a swing and set it up near you. You may have as long as an hour to make dinner, have a shower or watch television without a baby in your arms.

Loofah

NOTES

_____

_____

_____

_____

_____

_____

DATE --------------

Many mothers feel such love and devotion for their baby that they live in a constant state of terror. They know one thing for certain . . . if something were to happen to their baby, they would never survive it.

First, let's rush to remind ourselves that our children will be fine and still around long after they have lost most of their charm. Then, let's feel the awe at the bond between mothers and babies. It's a love so fierce it can literally make your heart hurt. Welcome to the Order of the Perpetually Vulnerable.

Notes

DATE --------------

If you are still breastfeeding, you may doubt this information, but it will ring true eventually: the breasts of women who have birthed babies will never regain their prepregnancy fullness and firmness. Think *National Geographic* for a visual cue. Anyone who tells you different is either a fluke of nature or neglecting to mention a certain plastic surgeon in her life.

Notes

DATE _____

It's never too early to learn not to waste time comparing your child's development with others. Everybody knows someone whose baby is a month younger than yours and already sleeps through the night. Later, it will be the baby who walks before yours does or is potty-trained in one day at eighteen months. Ignore it all. Someday, all of these kids will be working for your late-blooming genius.

NOTES

_____

_____

_____

_____

_____

_____

DATE _____

Are you breastfeeding? Have you had sex yet that was truly arousing, not just merciful?

Then you must be familiar with the 'car wash' phenomenon. Women with sensitive 'letdown' reflexes have been known to climax and spray milk simultaneously. Consider putting your nursing bra back on after the foreplay, and use extra pads.

Notes

_____

_____

_____

_____

_____

_____

DATE _____

New mothers often become environmental activists. They didn't mind living in air pollution themselves, but they put up a holler if their baby's precious lungs are vulnerable. Anyone lighting up a cigar risks personal injury, and I don't mean from the tobacco.

Notes

_____

_____

_____

_____

_____

_____

DATE _____

If you've already fallen behind or given up on the baby book, don't worry.

Look at it this way: odds are you'll never have time to do it for a sibling (easy for us to plan ahead), so it's not fair to do it for the firstborn. And if this is an only child, he will have no frame of reference. Are we Best Friends good at rationalization or what?

NOTES

DATE _____

If your feet got bigger during your pregnancy, and we're pretty sure they did, then about now you must be wondering when they are going to shrink back to their normal size. You can stop wondering because this bigger foot *is* your new normal size.

Look on the bright side . . . you have a great excuse to buy new shoes, and this foot growth usually happens only once in your reproductive life, even if you have ten more kids.

Notes

_____

_____

_____

_____

_____

_____

DATE _____

Now that you and your partner are officially 'grown up' (by virtue of being someone's parents), it is time to draft a will. If you don't legally state how you would want things to go if something were to happen to you, the courts decide. Horrifying concept, isn't it? About the courts, I mean.

Even if you have no great wealth to provide for, you must decide who would take care of your child if neither of you could. OK, stop crying. We don't have to talk about it any more today.

Notes

_____

_____

_____

_____

_____

_____

DATE _ _ _ _ _ _ _ _ _ _ _ _ _

You are not lacking in maternal instinct if the presence of other children close to your precious baby drives you crazy. You are completely correct in your opinion that children are perpetually moving, bacteria-producing threats to your infant's well-being, and that includes your own older children.

Notes

_____

_____

_____

_____

_____

_____

DATE _____

If you have been ill since the baby was born, then you know the deep, dark secret: if you're a mummy, it is a LUXURY to be too sick to get out of bed. In your child-free days, a silly little cold could be enough to send you straight for the couch, wrapped in a blanket. Now you have to be bleeding profusely before someone steps in and takes over for you. Unfortunately, the same phenomenon does not apply to your partner, who still turns into a baby as soon as his temperature soars to 99 degrees.

Notes

_____

_____

_____

_____

_____

_____

DATE --------------

Do not join a gym yet! Sure, you're sick and tired of looking chubby and flabby, but your salvation does not lie in a programme of muscle building. If you are still fat and you add muscle underneath, you will look twice as fat! Walk, walk, walk, up to sixty minutes a day if you can, until you are within five pounds of your desired weight, and then you can start going for the six-pack stomach and the sinewy triceps. (We can dream, can't we?)

Notes

DATE _____

You will have noticed early on in your pregnancy that your nipples got larger and darker; and especially if you're breastfeeding, they still are. About nine (ten) months after the birth they will return to their former circumference, but they probably will not go back to their old colour.

NOTES

_____

_____

_____

_____

_____

_____

DATE _____

Forgetfulness is a hallmark of motherhood. You can't count the number of times you've walked into a room to do something and entirely forgotten what it was you intended to do. It happens in shops, at work, everywhere. Get used to it . . . it just gets worse until it is replaced by senility.

Notes

_____

_____

_____

_____

_____

_____

DATE _____

Stop wasting your time with presoaks and scrubbing. Baby 'erp' stains their shirts, especially if they drink formula. You can recycle much of your infant's wardrobe with subsequent children, but those shirts and nightgowns just might be too yellow.

NOTES

_____

_____

_____

_____

_____

_____

DATE _____

Some mothers, usually women without full-time jobs or other children, believe in teaching newborns language through the use of flash cards . . . or worse, it is the father who is eager to give his baby a head start and he suggests that 'since you have some extra time on your hands', you should devote it to developing the mind of your baby, since you are both convinced she's a genius anyway.

It all sounds like a headache to us Best Friends, for both you and your barely focusing baby.

Skip the cards and take up singing to your baby . . . it's less pressure.

Notes

_____

_____

_____

_____

_____

_____

DATE _____

We spend most of our lives grateful that our mothers don't live with us, or even near us. But, when you become a mother, that dynamic can change. Your partner is probably back at work, and there you are, alone with a baby.

Reach out. You are not expected to do this all alone. If your mother-in-law hints that she might like to visit, send her a ticket (return) immediately, even if you think she doesn't approve of you. As the mother of her beloved grandchild, she will do anything for the baby. Ask for advice, accept it and know that she loves the baby nearly as much as you do.

NOTES

_____

_____

_____

_____

_____

_____

DATE ---------------

Meet other mums. Look into parent–baby groups at your church, community centre or among your Best Friends.

Not only does misery love company, but a forum for questions and concerns, as well as heaps of reassurance, goes miles in keeping a new mother sane. This is too big a job for you to do alone.

NOTES

DATE _____

I don't care whether you're a coal miner, a brain surgeon or a probation officer, there is no job harder than being a mother.

Other jobs allow you to sleep occasionally, they don't dictate what you can eat or drink, they don't expect you to offer your body as nourishment – and at other jobs, people occasionally say 'thank you'.

NOTES

_____

_____

_____

_____

_____

_____

DATE --------------

Are you afraid you might be going bald and are freaking out? Calm down, Best Friend, it happens to the best of us. One day, when you are shampooing, you notice hunks of hair coming out, and you begin to sweat, even though you are already wet.

When pregnant, your normal hair loss of a few strands a day stops, but, after the birth, your scalp releases the hair that it held on to during pregnancy. It can look quite dramatic, but don't rush to the doctor yet, because it will calm down long before other people notice a thing.

NOTES

86

Relax & Nap

DATE _____

'Nine (ten) months up, nine (ten) months down' is the Best Friends'
motto about pregnancy weight gain and loss. Please do not start fretting
now because you still have chubby thighs and a belly with the
consistency of bread dough. You are not supposed to be thin yet; you are
still pregnant, remember? The baby isn't in your tummy anymore, but
your body is still in an altered state.

Now, calm down and take a nap.

NOTES

_____

_____

_____

_____

_____

_____

DATE _____

Motherhood is a marathon, not a sprint. The key to finishing this race is conserving energy and setting a reasonable pace. Now is not the time to learn Chinese cooking or repaint the garage doors, even if those silly books and magazines insist all homemakers do it.

Consider yourself eminently productive if you and your baby have eaten, been bathed, put on clean clothes and watched *Oprah*.

Anything more is ludicrous.

Notes

_____
_____
_____
_____
_____
_____

DATE _____

Take this little bit of Best Friend wisdom and carry it with you for the rest
of your mothering days: you will never really know how good a mother
you have been. Even when you have a promising college graduate
sending you thrilling and literate letters from exciting places, you may
have another child of your womb, who was raised with all your love and
care, who collects roadkill and puts it in the freezer. No matter what, they
will continue to change inexplicably. As hard as it is to believe, studies
have proved you will love them anyway.

NOTES

_____

_____

_____

_____

_____

_____

TOP 10 REASONS WHY YOU'LL DO THIS ALL OVER AGAIN

10. MUMMIES' ALZHEIMER'S . . . YOU'VE ALREADY FORGOTTEN ALL THE WORST PARTS.

9. YOU'VE SPENT SO MUCH MONEY ON BABY STUFF, YOU NEED SEVERAL BABIES TO JUSTIFY THE EXPENSE.

8. IT'S A GOOD EXCUSE FOR NOT LOSING THOSE LAST FIFTEEN POUNDS.

7. YOU NEED ANOTHER BABY TO KEEP ALL THE GRANDPARENTS FROM FIGHTING OVER THE ONE YOU HAVE.

6. YOU ACTUALLY BELIEVED THAT BREASTFEEDING MOTHERS CAN'T GET PREGNANT.

5. YOU ARE SO TIRED THAT YOU COULDN'T REMEMBER IF YOU INSERTED YOUR DIAPHRAGM OR JUST CONSIDERED IT A GOOD IDEA.

4. YOU WANT THOSE GIGANTIC TITS BACK.

3. YOU KNOW WHAT THEY SAY ABOUT AN ONLY CHILD . . .

2. AN ADDICTION TO THE INTOXICATING SMELL FOUND IN THAT FOLD OF SKIN RIGHT WHERE THE BABY'S FAT LITTLE NECK MEETS ITS FAT LITTLE SHOULDER.

1. WINE.

FURTHER INFORMATION

Organizations

National Childbirth Trust

www.nctpregnancyandbabycare.com

0870 770 3236

Provides services and activities offering support in pregnancy, childbirth and early parenthood e.g. antenatal classes

Birth Resource Centre

www.birthresourcecentre.org.uk

0131 229 3667

A Scottish organization offering talks and classes to women and their families before and after childbirth

One Parent Families

www.oneparentfamilies.org.uk

020 7428 5400

Offers advice on the financial and social aspects of becoming a single parent. Contains advice on pregnancy as a single mother

Twins and Multiple Births Association

www.tamba.org.uk

0870 770 3305

Offers advice on parenting twins or more as well as events and holiday information

La Leche League Great Britain

www.laleche.org.uk

08450 120 2918

Organization promoting a better understanding of breastfeeding. Offers information and support via local groups. Also provides a telephone counselling service

The Breastfeeding Network

www.breastfeedingnetwork.org.uk

0870 900 9787

Offers information and support on breastfeeding, with support centres around the country

Day Care Trust

www.daycaretrust.org.uk

020 7739 2866

Organization offering advice on childcare

Independent Midwives Association

www.independentmidwives.org.uk

01483 821 104

Organization and website resource for enquiries and information on midwives. Includes a list of midwives by region

Doula

www.doula.org.uk

0871 433 3103

Network offering emotional and practical support to women before, during and after childbirth through personal visits from a 'Doula' or helper

Websites

www.babydirectory.com

020 8678 9000

Website offering advice on fashion, children's health, finding a nanny and much more. Gives an A-Z by region of services for pregnant women and mothers

www.readysteadybaby.com

Website offering information on pregnancy, childbirth and life in the few months after birth

www.forparentsbyparents.co.uk

Website aiming to give an honest view of parenting – 'even the grim bits'

www.baby-greenhouse.co.uk

Internet chat room for pregnant women and new mothers

www.babyworld.co.uk

Website offering up-to-date information on being a parent. Online discussion forums

www.caesarean.org.uk

Website offering research-based information and support on all aspects of caesareans

www.childbirth.org

Non-uk website offering articles and information on childbirth

www.sheilakitzinger.com

The website of writer, researcher and activist Sheila Kitzinger who explores women's experiences of childbirth

www.birthchoiceuk.com

Website designed to help women decide where to have their baby and who will look after them during labour and birth

www.drfoster.co.uk/birth

Website offering information on every hospital maternity unit in the UK with an analysis of the results

www.mumsnet.com

Online advice on how to find equipment and nappies etc. and other parenting tips

www.midwivesonline.com

Advice and support on all aspects of pregnancy and parenting

www.birthcentre.com

Website offering information on all the differing birthing options

www.mothersbliss.co.uk

Website for expectant mums and new families

www.ukparents.co.uk

Online articles and discussions covering all aspects of parenting

NOTES